INTRODUCING
ISSUES WITH
OPPOSING
VIEWPOINTS®

War

Lauri S. Friedman, *Book Editor*

GREENHAVEN PRESS
A part of Gale, Cengage Learning

GALE
CENGAGE Learning™

Detroit • New York • San Francisco • New Haven, Conn • Waterville, Maine • London

GALE
CENGAGE Learning

Christine Nasso, *Publisher*
Elizabeth Des Chenes, *Managing Editor*

© 2010 Greenhaven Press, a part of Gale, Cengage Learning

Gale and Greenhaven Press are registered trademarks used herein under license.

For more information, contact:
Greenhaven Press
27500 Drake Rd.
Farmington Hills, MI 48331-3535
Or you can visit our Internet site at gale.cengage.com

For product information and technology assistance, contact us at

Gale Customer Support, 1-800-877-4253
For permission to use material from this text or product, submit all requests online at www.cengage.com/permissions

Further permissions questions can be e-mailed to permissionrequest@cengage.com

Articles in Greenhaven Press anthologies are often edited for length to meet page requirements. In addition, original titles of these works are changed to clearly present the main thesis and to explicitly indicate the author's opinion. Every effort is made to ensure that Greenhaven Press accurately reflects the original intent of the authors. Every effort has been made to trace the owners of copyrighted material.

Cover image copyright © Ed Darach/Terra/Corbis.

LIBRARY OF CONGRESS CATALOGING-IN-PUBLICATION DATA

War / Lauri S. Friedman, book editor.
   p. cm. -- (Introducing issues with opposing viewpoints)
Includes bibliographical references and index.
ISBN 978-0-7377-4484-2 (hardcover)
1. War--Juvenile literature. 2. War--Causes--Juvenile literature. 3. War (Philosophy)--Juvenile literature. 4. War--Prevention--Juvenile literature.
I. Friedman, Lauri S.
  U21.2.W3585 2009
  355.02--dc22
                                    2009026387

Printed in the United States of America
1 2 3 4 5 6 7 13 12 11 10 09

Contents

Chapter 3: Can War Be Prevented?

Foreword

Indulging in a wide spectrum of ideas, beliefs, and perspectives is a critical cornerstone of democracy. After all, it is often debates over differences of opinion, such as whether to legalize abortion, how to treat prisoners, or when to enact the death penalty, that shape our society and drive it forward. Such diversity of thought is frequently regarded as the hallmark of a healthy and civilized culture. As the Reverend Clifford Schutjer of the First Congregational Church in Mansfield, Ohio, declared in a 2001 sermon, "Surrounding oneself with only like-minded people, restricting what we listen to or read only to what we find agreeable is irresponsible. Refusing to entertain doubts once we make up our minds is a subtle but deadly form of arrogance." With this advice in mind, Introducing Issues with Opposing Viewpoints books aim to open readers' minds to the critically divergent views that comprise our world's most important debates.

Introducing Issues with Opposing Viewpoints simplifies for students the enormous and often overwhelming mass of material now available via print and electronic media. Collected in every volume is an array of opinions that captures the essence of a particular controversy or topic. Introducing Issues with Opposing Viewpoints books embody the spirit of nineteenth-century journalist Charles A. Dana's axiom: "Fight for your opinions, but do not believe that they contain the whole truth, or the only truth." Absorbing such contrasting opinions teaches students to analyze the strength of an argument and compare it to its opposition. From this process readers can inform and strengthen their own opinions, or be exposed to new information that will change their minds. Introducing Issues with Opposing Viewpoints is a mosaic of different voices. The authors are statesmen, pundits, academics, journalists, corporations, and ordinary people who have felt compelled to share their experiences and ideas in a public forum. Their words have been collected from newspapers, journals, books, speeches, interviews, and the Internet, the fastest growing body of opinionated material in the world.

Introducing Issues with Opposing Viewpoints shares many of the well-known features of its critically acclaimed parent series, Opposing Viewpoints. The articles are presented in a pro/con format, allowing readers to absorb divergent perspectives side by side. Active reading questions preface each viewpoint, requiring the student to approach the material thoughtfully and carefully. Useful charts, graphs, and cartoons supplement each article. A thorough introduction provides readers with crucial background on an issue. An annotated bibliography points the reader toward articles, books, and Web sites that contain additional information on the topic. An appendix of organizations to contact contains a wide variety of charities, nonprofit organizations, political groups, and private enterprises that each hold a position on the issue at hand. Finally, a comprehensive index allows readers to locate content quickly and efficiently.

Introducing Issues with Opposing Viewpoints is also significantly different from Opposing Viewpoints. As the series title implies, its presentation will help introduce students to the concept of opposing viewpoints and learn to use this material to aid in critical writing and debate. The series' four-color, accessible format makes the books attractive and inviting to readers of all levels. In addition, each viewpoint has been carefully edited to maximize a reader's understanding of the content. Short but thorough viewpoints capture the essence of an argument. A substantial, thought-provoking essay question placed at the end of each viewpoint asks the student to further investigate the issues raised in the viewpoint, compare and contrast two authors' arguments, or consider how one might go about forming an opinion on the topic at hand. Each viewpoint contains sidebars that include at-a-glance information and handy statistics. A Facts About section located in the back of the book further supplies students with relevant facts and figures.

Following in the tradition of the Opposing Viewpoints series, Greenhaven Press continues to provide readers with invaluable exposure to the controversial issues that shape our world. As John Stuart Mill once wrote: "The only way in which a human being can make some approach to knowing the whole of a subject is by hearing what can be said about it by persons of every variety of opinion and studying all modes in which it can be looked at by every character of mind. No wise man ever acquired his wisdom in any mode but this." It is to this principle that Introducing Issues with Opposing Viewpoints books are dedicated.

Introduction

O n January 17, 1961, in his farewell address to the nation, President Dwight D. Eisenhower warned his fellow Americans of becoming a nation caught in a perpetual state of war: "We must guard against the acquisition of unwarranted influence, whether sought or unsought, by the military-industrial complex," he said. "The potential for the disastrous rise of misplaced power exists and will persist. We must never let the weight of this combination endanger our liberties or democratic processes."

The military-industrial complex of which Eisenhower warned is essentially a relationship between the people who start and manage wars—such as the military and the government—and the companies that make and sell the weapons and equipment with which wars are fought. Eisenhower and others saw the potential for this relationship to become all too self-serving: that is, war could come to be seen as "good for business" because it keeps so many businesses running and people employed, and thus war would become the preferred state of existence.

In the twenty-first century, many think of Eisenhower's warning when they realize that, according to the International Institute for Strategic Studies and the U.S. Department of Defense, in 2008 the nations of the world spent $1.47 trillion on their militaries. The United States outspent most of the other nations *combined*—it accounted for 48 percent of all military spending, investing $711 billion in its military in that year alone. The second highest spender was China, which lagged far behind the United States with $122 billion spent on its military.

But the United States was not always such a big military spender. Before World War I, the United States kept a small military in peaceful times. Large-scale spending was undertaken only in the event of an impending military conflict. However, when the United States entered World War II, it dedicated itself to fighting and winning against its enemies in Europe and Asia—and that meant spending. Indeed, during World War II the United States experienced the greatest military buildup since its birth as a nation. When the United States emerged victorious from the war, it also emerged with a first-class military whose strength was nearly unmatched by any other nation in the world.

The only other nation as strong as the United States after World War II was the Soviet Union. Immediately, the two nations began to vie for power and influence. It was because of this conflict—or cold war—that the United States did not demilitarize after the war, as it had in other peaceful times. In fact, over the course of the forty-five-year cold war with the Soviets, the United States built up its military with even more powerful weapons to prepare for the possibility of conflict with that empire. In this way the military-industrial complex became firmly entrenched in the national system.

While Americans widely agree that the United States needs some form of military to protect it from external threats, they disagree over how much money the military should get. At present, the military-industrial complex supports hundreds of thousands of jobs and keeps thousands of companies afloat. For example, in 2009 the *Washington Post* reported that about 7.5 percent of just the Washington, D.C., area's labor force is tied to military contracts—about 291,000 jobs in that area alone. Defense spending defies the wildest dreams of most Americans—according to the Web site MilitaryIndustrialComplex .com, which tracks military spending, in 2009 the United States had spent $59,649,153,607 on defense contracts by midyear. In just one day alone, on April 21, 2009, twelve contracts worth a total of $1,557,379,288 were awarded to various contractors.

Analysts like Carl Conetta of the Project on Defense Alternatives think this is too much. Conetta and others argue that the current threats Americans face cannot be defeated with a traditionally large military. Terrorists, for example, are capable of carrying out large-scale attacks on small, thousand-dollar budgets and in relative secrecy—tanks, missiles, and other high-cost military weapons are ineffective at disrupting such plans. Likewise, insurgents in Iraq or Afghanistan—small-scale terrorist-like fighters who use suicide bombers or other small-scale warfare techniques to inflict damage over time—are difficult to fight with a traditional army. Says Conetta, "Clearly, the flood of defense dollars has not purchased stability in either Iraq or Afghanistan, nor has it led to a general decrease in terrorist activity."[1] Conetta and others believe intelligence and clandestine operations are better for meeting these kinds of threats than a large, expensive military.

Yet others argue that now is no time to cut spending for America's armed forces. Indeed, as of 2009 America was committed to wars in both Iraq and Afghanistan and embroiled in the ongoing war on terrorism. What the American military needs most, say Heritage Foundation analysts James Jay Carafano and Mackenzie Eaglen, is not a cut in spending but a boost in spending. "Spending [more] on national defense will allow the U.S. to keep the nation and its service members properly trained, equipped, and ready," say Carafano and Eaglen. "Not spending enough on defense also creates the reality and perception of American weakness, which will increase risk, hinder economic growth, and lower stability in the world."[2]

How much the United States should spend on defense and what kind of military best meets the threats of the twenty-first century is an ongoing matter of debate and just one of the issues explored in *Introducing Issues with Opposing Viewpoints: War*. Readers will also consider arguments about what causes war, whether war is ever just, and whether war can be prevented. Readers will examine these issues in pro/con article pairs and form their own opinions on the nature and future of war and conflict.

Notes

1. Carl Conetta, "America Speaks Out: Is the United States Spending Too Much on Defense?" Project on Defense Alternatives Briefing Memo #41, Commonwealth Institute, March 26, 2007. www.comw .org/pda/0703bm41.html.

2. James Jay Carafano and Mackenzie Eaglen, "Four Percent for Freedom: Maintaining Robust National Security Spending," Executive Memorandum No. 1023, Heritage Foundation, April 10, 2007. www.heritage.org/Research/NationalSecurity/em1023.cfm.

Chapter 1

What Causes War?

Radical Islamic groups rally in Pakistan against the government.

Clashes Between Cultures Cause War

Jeff Jacoby

"There can't be much question that at this point in the war against radical Islam, the radicals are on the march."

In the following viewpoint Jeff Jacoby argues that radical Islam is responsible for violence and war all around the world. He cites actions such as kidnappings, bombings, and riots as proof that Muslim extremists seek to destroy the West and anyone else they view as their enemies. Jacoby argues that America must recognize this threat and not silently stand by the way that western European nations have. He urges Americans to realize they are in a clash of civilizations with radical Islam, a clash from which only one culture can emerge victorious.

Jacoby is a columnist for the *Boston Globe.* His articles have also appeared in the *Cleveland Jewish News,* where this viewpoint was originally printed.

AS YOU READ, CONSIDER THE FOLLOWING QUESTIONS:

1. What does Jacoby say women who do not wear headscarves are like to Sheik Taj al-Din Hilali?
2. Who did Islamic terrorists bomb in Thailand, according to the author?
3. What name does Jacoby give western Europe and why?

Jeff Jacoby, "Scenes from the Jihad—Not a Pretty Picture," *Cleveland Jewish News,* vol. 105, November 17, 2006, p. 10. Reproduced by permission.

A half-dozen snapshots from the global jihad:

Australia: Australia's foremost Muslim cleric triggers an uproar when he likens women who don't wear an Islamic headscarf to "uncovered meat" and blames them for attracting sexual predators.

"If you take out uncovered meat and place it outside on the street or in the garden or the park and the cats come and eat it," says Sheik Taj al-Din Hilali, "whose fault is it, the cats' or the uncovered meat's? If (the woman) was in her room, in her home, in her headscarf, no problem would have occurred."

Afghanistan: The kidnappers of Italian photojournalist Gabriele Torsello threaten to murder him unless Abdul Rahman, an Afghan Christian convert, is returned to Afghanistan and handed over to an Islamic court. Rahman lives in Italy, which granted him asylum earlier this year [2006] when he faced the death penalty under Afghanistan's sharia law for converting from Islam to Christianity.

Iran: The president of Iran calls Israel "a group of terrorists" and threatens to harm any country that supports the Jewish state. "This is an ultimatum," warns [President] Mahmoud Ahmadinejad, who has called for the elimination of Israel and the United States. "Don't complain tomorrow."

Days later, the deputy director of Iran's Atomic Energy Organization confirms another stride forward for the country's illicit nuclear program: With the injection of gas into a second cascade of centrifuges, Iran has doubled its uranium-enrichment capacity.

Violent Attacks by Islamists

Thailand: Islamist terrorists bomb a column of Buddhist monks as they collect offerings of food in Narathiwat, a city in southern Thailand. One person is killed; 12 are injured. The attack is the latest

A Clash of Civilizations

A 2008 poll of people in twenty-one countries found that most think Islam and the West are caught in a clash of civilizations that will lead to, or has already led to, war.

Are divisions between Muslim and Western worlds worsening?

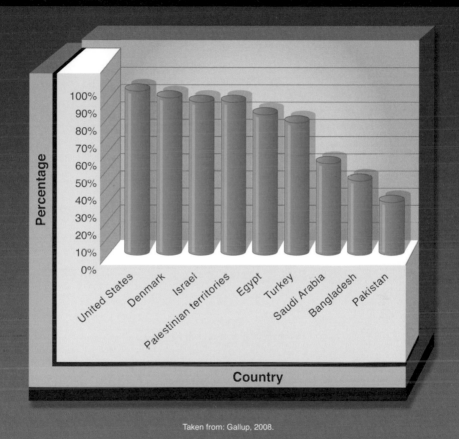

Taken from: Gallup, 2008.

in a bloody week that has included multiple shootings and another fatal bombing.

France: Another Muslim intifada [uprising against oppression] rages in France. Hundreds of cars are torched nightly and passenger buses set ablaze with Molotov cocktails. One such fire in Marseille leaves a 26-year-old woman in a coma with burns covering 70 percent of her body.

Thai police inspect the scene of a bombing by radical Islamic terrorists. The author contends that repeated bombings by these groups prove Islam is on the march to war.

"We are in a state of civil war, orchestrated by radical Islamists," says police union leader Michel Thoomis. "This is not a question of urban violence any more. It is an intifada, with stones and firebombs." So far [in 2006,] more than 2,500 police have been wounded in clashes with rioters.

Britain: In a "true Islamic state," sexually active homosexuals would be executed, says Arshad Misbahi, an imam in Manchester's Central Mosque. According to interviewer John Casson, the imam explains that while executions "might result in the deaths of thousands," they would be worthwhile "if this deterred millions from having sex and spreading disease."

Fighting Back Against Radical Islam

Not all the news is bad. NATO forces have recently killed scores of Taliban fighters in Afghanistan. Czech intelligence agents thwarted an Islamist plan to seize the Central Synagogue in Prague on Rosh Hashanah, hold the Jewish worshipers hostage, and then blowing up the building with its occupants.

A proposal to let Muslim taxi drivers at the Minneapolis–St. Paul International Airport refuse service to passengers carrying alcohol was scrapped in the wake of vehement public opposition. And the world's mightiest fighting force continues to kill Islamofascists in Iraq, currently the key battleground in the global jihad.

But there can't be much question that at this point in the war against radical Islam, the radicals are on the march. From Ahmadinejad's swagger, to Hezbollah's [an Islamic political and paramilitary group based in Lebanon] war on Israel, to the plot to blow up jetliners leaving London, our enemies are aggressive, relentless, and unequivocal in their determination to defeat us.

Meanwhile, Western Europe is turning into Eurabia before our eyes, as a fading native population with its effete secular culture of pacifism and relativism is superseded by a surging Muslim cohort. Most Muslims are not Islamists or terrorists, of course. However, most of them keep quiet in the face of the radical offensive. That is all the radicals need to keep driving the jihad [a holy war waged on behalf of Islam] forward.

America Must Wake Up

"If this country lets down its guard, it will be a fatal mistake," President [George W.] Bush said recently. Yet too many Americans seem unable to recognize the threat, or to believe that they, their liberties, and the lives of innumerable human beings are truly at stake in a deadly global war.

But radical Islam is not going away. Like Nazism and communism, it is (in Senator Rick Santorum's words) "an ideology that produces the systemic murder of innocents." Like those earlier totalitarianisms, it will go on murdering until it is crushed. Like them, it is impervious to appeasement and contemptuous of weakness. The longer Americans sleep, the farther the jihad advances.

EVALUATING THE AUTHOR'S ARGUMENTS:

Jeff Jacoby begins his viewpoint with a series of stories, or anecdotes. In your opinion, do these selected stories weaken his argument? Or do these stories help you visualize the culture clash he argues exists? Explain your opinion of what anecdotes offer persuasive essays like this one.

Clashes Between Cultures Do Not Cause War

"Arguing that there is a fundamental 'clash' between the United States and the Muslim World . . . rests on a number of false presumptions."

Almas Sayeed

In the following viewpoint Almas Sayeed argues that America and the West are not caught in a culture clash with the Muslim world. Sayeed explains that while some Muslims think negatively about the United States, many others find much to admire about Western civilization. Millions of Muslims live, work, and thrive in the West and have no cultural clash with Western people or institutions. According to Sayeed, perpetuating the myth of a clash between Islamic and Western cultures will actually lead to more war, violence, and misunderstanding. Sayeed warns against oversimplifying war and conflict, saying problems are more complicated than culture clash theories imply.

Sayeed is an economic policy analyst and member of the Faith and Progressive Policy Initiative at the Center for American

Almas Sayeed, "Who Is Winning in the 'Clash of Civilizations'?" Center for American Progress, September 15, 2006. Copyright © Center for American Progress. This material was created by the Center for American Progress, www.americanprogress.org.

Progress, a think tank that supports issues such as universal health care and clean energy.

AS YOU READ, CONSIDER THE FOLLOWING QUESTIONS:
1. What do historians of Islam point out, according to Sayeed?
2. According to the author, what are the three aspects of the West Muslims most admire?
3. What has been the work of the Muslim Public Affairs Council, as stated by the author?

Five years after the events of September 11th, the House International Relations Subcommittee on the Middle East and Central Asia held a hearing yesterday [September 14, 2006] entitled "Is There a Clash of Civilizations? Islam, Democracy and Central Asia Policy." The hearing plays on [political scientist] Samuel Huntington's fateful doctrine.[1] Rather than using the hearing to debate the existence of a cultural clash between the Muslim and non-Muslim World, the subcommittee used the time to prove that such a clash does in fact exist. The idea of a fundamental "clash," combined with violent images in the Middle East, has worked rhetorical wonders in alarming and confusing us into believing that "they" hate "us" because of our freedom, liberty, and democracy. Such language that treats differences between the Muslim and non-Muslim world as an epic battle plays right into the hands of those like Osama bin Laden, who have built their followings on a similar worldview.

The hearing proved that the battle for "hearts and minds" has as much to do with language as it does specific policies. While Osama bin Laden argues that Muslims around the world are under threat of eradication from Western countries and must fight for their survival, the Chair of the House Subcommittee, Rep. [Ileana] Ros-Lehtinen (R-FL) writes that we are facing an enemy determined to "destroy Western Civilization and the principles upon which it is based." Other panelists, representing such "diverse" institutions as *The*

1. Political scientist Samuel Huntington theorized that, after the Cold War, future wars would be based on clashes between civilizations.

Washington Times and the Hudson Institute highlighted evidence to prove there is an irresolvable clash, including polling data showing that the U.S. is viewed unfavorably throughout much of the Muslim World. Arguments by ideologues on both sides of the conflict paint "the other" as extremist for political gain, using language of "fear" to gain new recruits.

The Falsehoods of a U.S.-Muslim Clash

There clearly is evidence of a real threat from those willing to engage in violence. Yet arguing that there is a fundamental "clash" between the United States and the Muslim World suggests that the tensions

An Iranian woman shows her finger stamped with ink after voting in the June 12, 2009, presidential election. Many Muslims admire Western institutions such as democracy and gender equality.

are natural and irresolvable—not largely political—and rests on a number of false presumptions.

The argument presumes that there are basic Islamic principles that fundamentally oppose Western Civilization as we know it today. The argument also suggests that an extremist interpretation of Islam—one that uses the religion to justify acts of violence—is practiced and embraced by the majority of Muslims throughout the world. Finally, it ignores examples of Muslim communities living in harmony in the West.

More comprehensive analysis suggests that there is more to the story than a simple and fundamental "clash." Historians of Islam point out that there is little opposition between the basic principles within Islam and life within Western countries. American-Muslim advocates repeatedly emphasize that when Western leaders and media use terms like "jihadist" [one who advocates a holy war waged on behalf of Islam] and Islamic Fascism, they bolster the Islamic legitimacy of terrorists. This elevates the voice of extremists and drowns out those who oppose using the religion for violent ends. Such language may help garner support for "national security" policies like the post-9/11 "Special Registration" program for Muslim immigrant men between 18 and 40 years old that ultimately yielded zero terrorists, but does little to help us in the struggle to understand and end terrorists' acts of violence.

Muslims Admire Many Facets of the West

These presumptions also assume that the majority of Muslims are opposed to anything associated with the West and practice an extremist version of Islam. Yet a new Gallup World Study coordinated by Islamic scholar and Georgetown University professor John L. Esposito surveying much of the Middle East and Muslim World, yielded different results. The majority of respondents

Cultural Differences Do Not Need to Cause War

A global poll of citizens in twenty-seven countries (including the United States) found that the majority of people think culture is not to blame for tensions between countries. The majority also think it is possible for Islam and the West to solve their differences peacefully.

Cause of Tensions Between Islam and the West

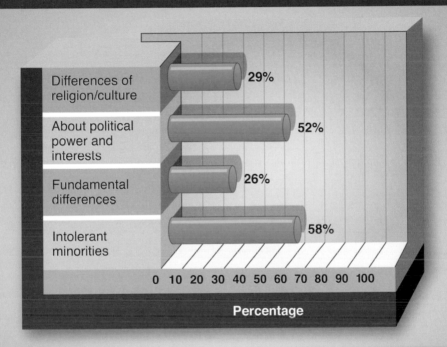

Views of the Relationship Between Muslim and Western Cultures

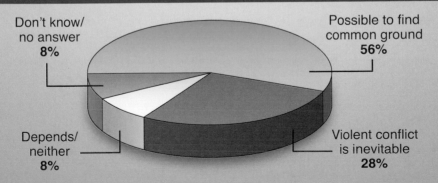

Taken from: BBC World Service, 2007.

labeled themselves as "moderates." They expressed an unfavorable opinion of the United States, but this did not translate to unfavorable opinions to all Western countries, such as those in Europe. This suggests that their unfavorable opinion has more to do with the United States' policies than Western civilizations as a whole.

Self-labeled "moderates" and "extremists," when asked what they admired most about the West, had the top three identical responses: technology; the West's value system of hard work, self-responsibility, rule of law, and cooperation; and its fair political systems, democracy, respect for human rights, freedom of speech, and gender equality. Although the majority clearly deplores the U.S.'s imposition of democracy in Muslim countries, a significantly higher percentage of extremists over moderates (50 versus 35 percent) believe that "moving towards greater governmental democracy" will foster progress in the Arab/Muslim world. This suggests less a "clash" of civilization and more of a deep opposition to the U.S.'s unilateralism [policies that support one-sided action] in the Middle East.

Many Muslims Call the West Home

The suggestion that there is a fundamental "clash" between Islam and the West overlooks the significant number of Muslims who now call Western countries, like the United States, home. American-Muslim communities continue to embrace both their Western and Muslim identities—destabilizing the assumption that these are mutually exclusive. Moreover, advocacy organizations like the Muslim Public Affairs Council have worked tirelessly with authorities to counter extremism within religious institutions and prevent another terrorist attack perpetrated by self-identified Muslim terrorists.

Yesterday's hearing largely overlooked the complexity of both the Muslim world and the West. However, Democratic committee member, Rep. [Gary] Ackerman (D-NY) and Steven Simon of the Council on Foreign Relations, did take the time to note that using generalizations and a language of a fundamental "clash" to shore up support for ineffective counter-terrorism policies will not win the struggle against terrorists or decrease the number of recruits for Osama bin Laden.

We must remember to be purposeful in our use of language and our counter-terrorism strategy in order to delegitimate those who use religious doctrine to justify their irreverent acts.

EVALUATING THE AUTHOR'S ARGUMENTS:

In this viewpoint Almas Sayeed argues that overall, Muslims do not hate Western civilization and are not interested in pursuing war with it. What evidence does he use to support this argument? Is his argument convincing? Explain why or why not.

Climate Change May Not Cause War

Nils Petter Gleditsch, Ragnhild Nordås, and Idean Salehyan

"The link between climate change and conflict is unclear."

The connection between climate change and war is largely unsubstantiated, Nils Petter Gleditsch, Ragnhild Nordås, and Idean Salehyan argue in the following viewpoint. According to the authors, although changes in the environment can lead to serious problems such as famine, floods, and water shortages, little evidence connects these changes to violent conflict. They argue that evidence showing climate change will cause conflict is weak, scarce, and overreported. Furthermore, they complain that pieces of evidence that do point to climate change conflict are too easily bounced around from report to report, repeated without any critical analysis or scrutiny. They conclude it is too early to know if climate change will cause war and caution against blindly repeating this untested warning.

Gleditsch is a professor of political science at the Norwegian University of Science and Technology. Nordås is a research fellow

Nils Petter Gleditsch, Ragnhild Nordås, and Idean Salehyan, "Introduction and Challenges: Environment-Induced Migration," *Climate Change and Conflict: The Migration Link,* May 2007, pp. 1, 3–5, 7. Copyright © by the International Peace Academy, 2007. Reproduced by permission.

at the Centre for the Study of Civil War at the International Peace Research Institute. Salehyan is an assistant professor of political science at the University of North Texas. The International Peace Academy has renamed itself the International Peace Institute since the original publication of this viewpoint.

AS YOU READ, CONSIDER THE FOLLOWING QUESTIONS:
1. What do Egbert Sondorp and Preeti Patel think about the connection between climate change and war, according to the authors?
2. According to the authors, which scholars argue that sharing water resources usually results in cooperation rather than conflict?
3. What problem do the authors have with sources used in the Stern Review?

In October 2003, a report to the US Department of Defense received wide public attention for presenting a grim future scenario with warring states and massive social disturbance as a result of dramatic climate change. Although not intended to be a prediction, the authors nevertheless argued the plausibility of a scenario for rapid climate change which could result in a significant drop in the human carrying capacity of the earth's environment—food, water, and energy shortages, as well as extreme weather patterns. In turn, resource constraints and environmental damage could lead to geopolitical destabilization, skirmishes and even war.

A Weak Connection

Similar warnings can be found in numerous media statements and policy documents. The Christian Aid charity warns that 184 million people could die in Africa alone as a result of climate change before the end of the twenty-first century, through floods, famine, drought, and conflict. Similarly, Oxfam [a group of organizations that work together to fight poverty, hunger and injustice] relates climate change to droughts in northern Kenya, in turn leading to conflict between the Turkhana pastoralists and their neighbors. The German Environment Ministry finds that "evidence is mounting that the adverse effects of climate change can, particularly by interaction with a number of socioeconomic factors, contribute to an increasing potential for conflict." And in October 2006, the UK Treasury-commissioned *Stern Review* argued that climate change is likely to cause additional hundreds of millions to suffer hunger, water shortages, and coastal flooding. Although the report focused most directly on the economic consequences of climate change, it also foresaw mass migration and conflict in parts of the developing world.

However, the link made between climate change and violent conflict that appears so frequently in the media and political discourse is rarely substantiated with direct empirical evidence. Some scholars, such as Jon Barnett and Neil Adger, caution that the link between climate change and conflict is not well established. Egbert Sondorp and Preeti Patel argue that both climate change and conflict may produce serious health consequences, but that there is insufficient evidence that climate change leads to violent conflict.

In this [viewpoint] we review the current state of knowledge regarding climate change and violent conflict, paying special attention to the influential Intergovernmental Panel on Climate Change (IPCC) reports. We find that much of the literature is speculative and difficult to substantiate given data constraints. Indeed, current debates frequently focus on *possible* scenarios in the future, which are inherently difficult to test. . . .

Scattered Comments from Weak Sources

The IPCC finds that changes in global climate and atmospheric composition are likely to have an impact on ecosystems and economic sectors, such as forests, wetlands, and agriculture, with significant impacts on socioeconomic systems. In conjunction with other global changes, such as population growth and migration, the degradation of natural resources is likely to hinder increases in agricultural productivity and make it more difficult to satisfy the growing world demand for food. Developing countries are particularly vulnerable because of greater reliance on climate sensitive sectors, such as agriculture. Poverty also prevents long-term planning and provisioning at the household level. People and societies with poor finances and technical ability are less likely to be able to meet the challenge of climate change.

Scarce Resources Can Be Shared

Even if climate change causes resources to become scarce, countries may not go to war over them. Many of the world's rivers, for example, are peacefully shared by many countries.

Number of Countries That Share the River Basin	International Basins
3	Asi (Orontes), Awash, Cavally, Cestos, Chiloango, Dnieper, Dniester, Drin, Ebro, Essequibo, Gambia, Garonne, Gash, Geba, Har Us Nur, Hari (Harirud), Helmand, Hondo, Ili (Kunes He), Incomati, Irrawaddy, Juba-Shibeli, Kemi, Lake Prespa, Lake Titicaca-Poopo System, Lempa, Maputo, Maritsa, Maroni, Moa, Neretva, Ntem, Ob, Oueme, Pasvik, Red (Song Hong), Rhone, Ruvuma, Salween, Schelde, Seine, St. John, Sulak, Torne (Tornealven), Tumen, Umbeluzi, Vardar, Volga, and Zapaleri
4	Amur, Daugave, Elbe, Indus, Komoe, Lake Turkana, Limpopo, Lotagipi Swamp, Narva, Oder (Odra), Ogooue, Okavango, Orange, Po, Pu-Lun-T'o, Senegal, and Struma
5	La Plata, Neman, and Vistula (Wista)
6	Aral Sea, Ganges-Brahmaputra-Meghna, Jordan, Kura-Araks, Mekong, Tarim, Tigris and Euphrates (Shatt al Arab), and Volta
8	Amazon and Lake Chad
9	Rhine and Zambezi
10	Nile
11	Congo and Niger
17	Danube

In addition to national wealth, political institutions are also likely to affect the adaptive capacity of societies. Possible coping mechanisms include moving settlements away from coastal regions, improving water conservation in drought-affected areas, and creating infrastructure in cities expected to face population inflows from affected regions. Poor, authoritarian, and corrupt states that are not responsive to the needs of their citizens are unlikely to implement needed reforms. Reforms such as population relocation, energy conservation, and technological change may be politically costly in the short-term even if they provide long-term benefits. This time-inconsistency problem may require institutional changes that facilitate long-term planning and coordination at the international level.

The IPCC reports make only scattered comments about violent conflict as a consequence of climate change and these are largely based on secondary and politicized sources. While violent conflict may indeed be related to environmental changes, the few systematic studies show mixed evidence. Moreover, several mitigating factors are likely to complicate the relationship between climate change and conflict.

The authors of this viewpoint point to recent reports from the Intergovernmental Panel on Climate Change (IPCC) that downplay the conflict-causing effects of climate change.

Evidence Is Repeated Without Critical Analysis

One concrete link between climate change and violent conflict is suggested by the TAR [Third Assessment Report], which observes that "much has been written about the potential for international conflict (hot or cold) over water resources." The report comments that a change in water availability has the potential to induce conflict between different users. But such disputes need not be violent; they could even stimulate cooperation. The sources cited by the IPCC provide weak support for the idea of conflict over scarce water resources. The writings of Peter Gleick, Michael Klare, and others suggest a potential for water wars, but other scholars such as Peter Beaumont and Aaron Wolf argue that cooperation generally trumps conflict in handling shared water resources. Statistical studies have found that neighboring countries that share rivers experience low-level interstate conflict somewhat more frequently, but that they also tend to cooperate more. Whether conflict or cooperation will dominate is not a simple function of scarcity but depends on other variables such as mediation and dispute resolution mechanisms, the nature of property rights, and the ability to enforce agreements.

> **FAST FACT**
>
> Political scientist Idean Salehyan has pointed out that between 1989 and 2002—a period that saw an increase in global temperatures—some one hundred armed conflicts came to an end.

The overall impression from the IPCC report is that the link between climate change and conflict is unclear. Where such a link is mentioned, it is weakly substantiated with evidence. The *Stern Review* on the economics of climate change invites the same characterization. Its references to how conflict "may" occur as a result of climate change are mostly based on second-hand sources of the same nature as those used by the IPCC. The expected causal link from climate change to conflict seems to be cited uncritically from one source to the next. . . .

Weak and Faulty Results

There is some limited statistical evidence to suggest that environmental problems have led to conflict in the past. A frequently cited study by Wenche Hauge and Tanja Ellingsen found a positive link between environmental degradation and violence; while they suggest that this effect is quite small, future climate change may make environmental stress a more substantively significant predictor of violence. The Phase II Report of the US State Failure Task Force concluded that the link is weak and a recent study by Ole Magnus Theisen failed to replicate the Hauge and Ellingsen results. . . .

The link between climate change, migration, and conflict remains conjectural. Because it is difficult to isolate different causes of migration, it is unclear whether specific population movements have occurred as a direct result of environmental stresses rooted in climatic shift. There is good evidence linking conflict and emigration in sending areas and immigration and conflict in receiving areas. On the other hand, there is a lack of consensus and systematic data on the effects of climate change on migration and on the effect of climate-induced migration on conflict. Clearly identifying the sources of environmentally-induced migration and environmental conflicts is a difficult, yet much needed endeavor.

EVALUATING THE AUTHORS' ARGUMENTS:

In this viewpoint the authors argue that it is unclear whether climate change will cause conflict. Do you agree with this perspective? Why or why not? Explain your answer using evidence from the text you have just read.

Nations Go to War over Natural Resources

"All major states have now realized that petroleum and natural gas are . . . the driving force behind the coming conflicts."

Erich Follath

The growing demand for oil and gas can lead to war, Erich Follath asserts in the following viewpoint. Follath warns that oil is becoming more scarce while more nations are using increasing amounts of it. As the supply goes down and the demand goes up, Follath predicts countries will compete over this finite resource, even going to war over it. Already, says Follath, oil was a major reason why the United States went to war against Iraq. He further points out that the United States is facing potential problems with Venezuela, another major supplier of oil, which could lead to unrest and other problems. Follath concludes that in the coming years, the world is likely to see an increase in wars over natural resources like oil.

Follath is a writer for the German news magazine *Spiegel*, from which this viewpoint was taken.

S hould the world be trembling in fear? Should everyone be afraid that gas and heating will soon no longer be affordable? Concern over such issues is certainly spreading in Germany, a country whose energy security is good compared to many others. Should we shiver with fear of anticipated bloodshed over resource allocation? The superpower China is hunting these resources especially aggressively. Should we fear the war that comes from the cold?

Good News and Bad News About Oil
The good news is that it's improbable, despite all the dangers and bottlenecks, that fossil fuels will become the much cited unaffordable "black gold" overnight, or that they will even no longer be available in sufficient quantities. Besides, human inventiveness has always been able to discover or invent new energy sources.

The bad news is that the age of cheap oil and natural gas is definitely over. At the very least, the next generation will be bitterly punished for our reckless overconsumption of fossil fuels. Renewable energies and energy efficiency together won't be enough to cover the shortfall, either. In the long-term, even if renewable resources like solar power, wind power and biomass—which are urgently needed—are added into the energy mix with oil, natural gas, coal and nuclear energy, they will still only be able to cover one-quarter of the energy needs of industrialized nations. That's the best-case scenario.

Ideological trench fights over secure fuels aside, most reputable scientists agree that the historical "peak" of oil production will be reached in five to 10 years, despite improvements in drilling technology and the expansion of production to include oil shales and oil sands, which are difficult to process. From that point on, oil production will head downhill—despite increasing worldwide demand. . . .

Oil Is the Reason for War

All major states have now realized that petroleum and natural gas are of existential strategic significance. They are the driving force behind the coming conflicts. That's why the world's powerful stake the claims wherever vital reserves of resources can be found—by force of arms or through aggressive diplomacy. . . .

A U.S. soldier stands guard inside the Baiji oil refinery in Iraq. The author contends that oil was a major reason the United States went to war against Iraq.

Oil as a Foreign Policy Issue

A strategy paper commissioned by the [George W.] Bush administration and issued in May 2001 paints a sombre picture of the global energy situation, warning of the prospects for serious US energy deficits and energy dependence. The conclusion drawn is that questions related to "American energy supply security" should be given a high "priority" in US foreign policy. Soon after the paper was issued, [Vice President Dick] Cheney formulated the same message in more precise terms: He warned that [Iraqi president] Saddam Hussein was striving for hegemony in the Gulf region and might succeed in bringing a substantial part of the world's energy reserves under his control. The terrorist attacks of 9/11 and the almost 3,000 victims who died in New York's World Trade Center and in the Pentagon then dramatically revealed the US's vulnerability.

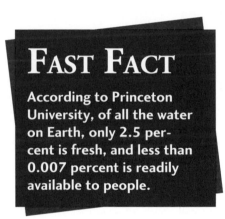

FAST FACT

According to Princeton University, of all the water on Earth, only 2.5 percent is fresh, and less than 0.007 percent is readily available to people.

Shortly before the US invasion of Iraq, Lawrence Lindsey, one of Bush's leading economic advisors, said that "the key issue is oil" and that "a regime change in Iraq would facilitate an increase in world oil." By and large, however, US politicians avoided making the obvious connection between a preemptive strike and resources.

Oil Drove War in Iraq

Other motives may have played a role as well: the fear of Saddam Hussein's weapons of mass destruction (a fear either imagined or rhetorically induced), or the desire to create a counterbalance to other authoritarian governments in the region—a kind of beachhead of democracy in the Middle East. But most of all, the US had what former CIA strategist Kenneth Pollack has called a "vital interest" in guaranteeing its energy supply and avoiding "possible blackmail" from hostile countries in the Persian Gulf. According to Pollack, only an idiot would fail to understand why Bush and company are in Iraq: "It's the oil, stupid!"

The Coming Water Wars

The world's freshwater is not evenly distributed around the world. As populations rise and water becomes scarce, experts worry nations will increasingly go to war over this precious resource.

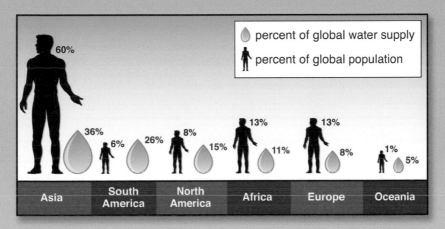

Taken from: Princeton University, United Nations, UNESCO, the *Montreal Gazette*, and the *New York Times*.

The US went on to suffer bitter setbacks in Iraq. And now [2006] the country is facing a possible confrontation with Iran, one in which its options don't look particularly promising. Add to that a possible long-term confrontation with China and the picture that emerges is far from pretty, at least from the White House's perspective. Despite Republican majorities in both the Senate and the Congress, Bush hasn't even been able to push through plans for oil extraction in the Arctic National Wildlife Refuge in Alaska.

The Complicated Relationship with Venezuela

Then, of course, there's that new troublemaker in the neighborhood, just four hours from Texas by plane, in South America, the US's back-yard. He's making a name for himself as George W. Bush's opponent, and the control he wields over substantial amounts of oil permits him to subject the US president to more than the occasional pinprick. *Forbes* magazine recently described Hugo Chavez, the 51-year-old president of Venezuela as "Oil's New Mr. Big."

Chavez provokes whenever and wherever he can. Speaking at the Caracas counter-summit he organized to coincide with the World Economic Forum Davos, at the end of January [2006], Chavez pulled no punches, calling George W. Bush "the greatest terrorist on earth" and the Bush administration "the most perverse, murderous and immoral government in history." He's even threatening to boycott the US by cutting off Venezuela's oil shipments to that country.

Using Oil as a Weapon

That's one reality. The other can be studied in Punto Fijo off the Caribbean coast. Punto Fijo is Venezuela's main oil port, where large vessels are filled up with the precious substance after it has been extracted from nearby Lake Maracaibo. Half a dozen oil tankers glisten in the bluish-green water, devouring 36,000 barrels every hour—each complete cargo load is worth $50 million. The most frequent destinations of these ships are Port Everglades, Baltimore and Boston. And when they have arrived and been cleared of their cargo, they immediately head back—every minute counts for big business.

The US is the main importer of Venezuelan oil; business is going smoothly; and the volume of business transactions is increasing. But the mutual dependence of Venezuela and the US is increasing too. Left-wing populist Chavez is dependent on billions in revenues from Venezuela's petroleum company PDVSA, which was nationalized in 1976, prior to Chavez coming to power. More than half of Venezuela's natural resources go to its large northern neighbor, and Chavez's Venezuela is one of the US's main oil suppliers, along with Canada, Mexico and Saudi Arabia.

Chavez uses the petrodollars from his dealings with the abhorred "Gringoland" to finance his army as well as the social welfare programs he has introduced for the neediest of his compatriots. The teacher's son sees himself as a latter-day Simon Bolivar [a nineteenth-century South American general who defeated the Spaniards in battle], as a liberator from colonialism. And in his view, the US of today has taken the place of the Spaniards of the 19th century. Chavez has taken it upon himself to unify the entire continent. In many parts of Latin America he has, in fact, succeeded his friend and advisor, Cuban revolutionary hero [and president] Fidel Castro, as the "hero of the street." . . .

The Conflict Is Coming

The enemy to the south has started to worry US politicians. The Senate Committee for Foreign Affairs has commissioned an urgent Emergency Plan to deal with the possibility that no more petroleum arrives from Venezuela. The USA have built up sufficient reserves to deal with such a scenario. But they would still be hard hit if their main supplier were to leave them in the lurch. There are barely any reserves on the global petroleum market that the USA could fall back on. If Venezuela cut off its oil supplies to the USA, oil prices would rise by at least 15 percent and cause considerable unrest, Washington's unofficial parliamentary report predicted in mid-June [2006].

The rise and fall of nations will involve considerable power shifts during the coming years. The USA aren't likely to be the winners of the coming conflicts over natural resources.

> **EVALUATING THE AUTHOR'S ARGUMENTS:**
>
> In this viewpoint Eric Follath warns that dwindling national resources will cause nations to go to war. In your opinion, are such wars inevitable? Can you think of ways in which countries might avoid such wars? Name at least one way in which the United States might avoid going to war over national resources.

Nations Do Not Always Go to War over Natural Resources

Aaron T. Wolf, Annika Kramer, Alexander Carius, and Geoffrey D. Dabelko

"No nations have gone to war specifically over water resources for thousands of years."

In the following viewpoint Aaron T. Wolf, Annika Kramer, Alexander Carius, and Geoffrey D. Dabelko argue that scarce natural resources do not always cause war. They reject recent concerns of scientists and political leaders that dwindling water supplies will cause nations to go to war. They point out several examples in which nations—even those that are enemies—have come to agreements about sharing water resources in their area, and they claim that overwhelmingly, competition over such resources has led to cooperation rather than conflict. The authors conclude that scarce resources need not necessarily contribute to violence and war, and policy makers should stop warning about this danger.

Wolf is professor of geography in the Department of Geosciences at Oregon State University and director of the Transboundary Freshwater Dispute Database. Kramer is a research fellow, and Carius is director of Adelphi Research in Berlin. Dabelko is the director of the Environmental Change and Security Program at the Woodrow Wilson International Center for Scholars in Washington, D.C.

AS YOU READ, CONSIDER THE FOLLOWING QUESTIONS:
1. How many countries do the authors say peacefully share the Danube river basin?
2. In the last fifty years, how many water disputes do the authors say have involved violence? How many outside of the Middle East?
3. What do the authors say is dangerous about "water wars warnings"?

"Water wars are coming!" the newspaper headlines scream. It seems obvious—rivalries over water have been the source of disputes since humans settled down to cultivate food. Even our language reflects these ancient roots: "rivalry" comes from the Latin *rivalis*, or "one using the same river as another." Countries or provinces bordering the same river (known as "riparians") are often rivals for the water they share. As the number of international river basins (and impact of water scarcity) has grown so do the warnings that these countries will take up arms to ensure their access to water. In 1995, for example, World Bank Vice President Ismail Serageldin claimed that "the wars of the next century will be about water."

Nations Almost Never Fight over Water

These apocalyptic warnings fly in the face of history: no nations have gone to war specifically over water resources for thousands of years. International water disputes—even among fierce enemies—are resolved peacefully, even as conflicts erupt over other issues. In fact, instances of cooperation between riparian nations outnumbered conflicts by more than two to one between 1945 and 1999. Why?

The author points to long-standing agreements held by the seventeen countries that share the Danube river basin to show that nations can peacefully share natural resources.

Because water is so important, nations cannot afford to fight over it. Instead, water fuels greater interdependence. By coming together to jointly manage their shared water resources, countries can build trust and prevent conflict. Water can be a negotiating tool, too: it can offer a communication lifeline connecting countries in the midst of crisis. Thus, by crying "water wars," doomsayers ignore a promising way to help *prevent* war: cooperative water resources management.

Of course, people compete—sometime violently—for water. Within a nation, users—farmers, hydroelectric dams, recreational users, environmentalists—are often at odds, and the probability of a mutually acceptable solution falls as the number of stakeholders rises. Water is never the single—and hardly ever the major—cause of conflict. But it can exacerbate existing tensions. History is littered with examples of violent water conflicts: just as Californian farmers bombed pipelines moving water from Owens Valley to Los Angeles in the early 1900s, Chinese farmers in Shandong clashed with police in 2000 to protest government plans to divert irrigation water to cities and industries. But these conflicts usually break out *within* nations. International rivers are a different story.

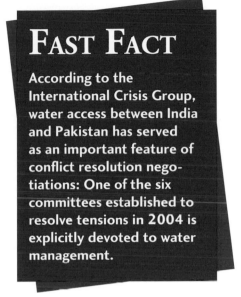

FAST FACT

According to the International Crisis Group, water access between India and Pakistan has served as an important feature of conflict resolution negotiations: One of the six committees established to resolve tensions in 2004 is explicitly devoted to water management.

Countries Have Lots of Practice Sharing Water

The world's 263 international river basins cover 45.3 percent of Earth's land surface, host about 40 percent of the world's population, and account for approximately 60 percent of global river flow. And the number is growing, largely due to the "internationalization" of basins through political changes like the breakup of the Soviet Union, as well as improved mapping technology. Strikingly, territory in 145 nations falls within international basins, and 33 countries are located almost entirely within these basins. As many as 17 countries share one river basin, the Danube.

Contrary to received wisdom, evidence shows this interdependence does not lead to war. Researchers at Oregon State University compiled a dataset of every reported interaction (conflictive or cooperative) between two or more nations that was driven by water in the last half century. They found that the rate of cooperation overwhelms the incidence of acute conflict. In the last 50 years, only 37 disputes

Nations Can Share Resources Peacefully

Since 1946, nations have handled transboundary water sources in many ways—but never with war. Verbal and nonmilitary agreements are most often used to sort out how to share water that flows across national borders.

State-to-State Water Interactions in Transboundary Basins, 1946–1999

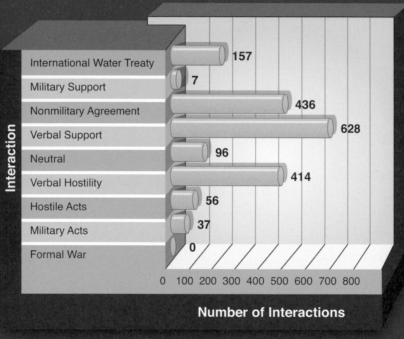

Taken from: Aaron Wolf et al., "Water Can Be a Pathway to Peace, Not War," Woodrow Wilson International Center, July 2006.

involved violence, and 30 of those occurred between Israel and one of its neighbors.

Outside of the Middle East, researchers found only 5 violent events while 157 treaties were negotiated and signed. The total number of water-related events between nations also favors cooperation: the 1,228 cooperative events dwarf the 507 conflict-related events. Despite the fiery rhetoric of politicians—aimed more often at their own constituencies than at the enemy—most actions taken over water are mild. Of all the events, 62 percent are verbal, and more than two-thirds of these were not official statements.

Even Enemies Share Resources Peacefully

Simply put, water is a greater pathway to peace than conflict in the world's international river basins. International cooperation around water has a long and successful history; some of the world's most vociferous enemies have negotiated water agreements. The institutions they have created are resilient, even when relations are strained. The Mekong Committee, for example, established by Cambodia, Laos, Thailand, and Vietnam in 1957, exchanged data and information on the river basin throughout the Vietnam War.

Israel and Jordan held secret "picnic table" talks to manage the Jordan River starting in 1953, even though they were officially at war from 1948 until the 1994 treaty. The Indus River Commission survived two major wars between India and Pakistan. And all 10 Nile Basin riparian countries are currently involved in senior government–level negotiations to develop the basin cooperatively, despite the verbal battles conducted in the media. Riparians will endure such tough, protracted negotiations to ensure access to this essential resource and its economic and social benefits.

Southern African countries signed a number of river basin agreements while the region was embroiled in a series of wars in the 1970s and 1980s, including the "people's war" in South Africa and civil wars in Mozambique and Angola. These complex negotiations produced rare moments of peaceful cooperation. Now that most of the wars and the apartheid era have ended, water management forms one of the foundations for cooperation in the region, producing one of the first protocols signed within the Southern African Development Community (SADC).

Stop Panicking over Resource Wars

Today, more than ever, it is time to stop propagating threats of "water wars" and aggressively pursue a water peacemaking strategy. Why?

- "Water wars" warnings force the military and other security groups to take over negotiations and push out development partners, like aid agencies and international financial institutions.

- Water management offers an avenue for peaceful dialogue between nations, even when combatants are fighting over other issues.
- Water management builds bridges between nations, some with little experience negotiating with each other, such as the countries of the former Soviet Union.
- Water cooperation forges people-to-people or expert-to-expert connections, as demonstrated by the transboundary water and sanitation projects Friends of the Earth Middle East conducts in Israel, Jordan, and Palestine.
- A water peacemaking strategy can create shared regional identities and institutionalize cooperation on issues larger than water.

EVALUATING THE AUTHORS' ARGUMENTS:

In this viewpoint the authors argue that competition over natural resources does not necessarily lead to war. In the previous viewpoint, Erich Follath warns of the opposite. After reading both viewpoints, with which perspective do you agree? Why? Cite evidence from the texts in your answer, and explain why you think the authors arrived at different conclusions on the matter.

Religion Contributes to War

Economist

> "Faith is once again prolonging conflict."

The magazine *Economist* contends in the following viewpoint that religion is often a motivating factor in wars and other violent conflicts. The author points out that violent conflict is often driven by religious ideology and imagery. Politicians throughout the world, including in the United States, increasingly frame conflict in religious terms, labeling enemies as "evil," "godless," or "wicked." Furthermore, religious convictions convince people they are righteous in their battles and make it difficult to negotiate peacefully with them. The author points to several conflicts that are influenced, if not driven, by religion. They conclude that religion need not be a violence-triggering force when it is nurtured in peaceful, constructive contexts. They urge all nations to find a way to deal with religious grievances that often become violent.

Economist is a weekly magazine that focuses on international political and financial issues.

AS YOU READ, CONSIDER THE FOLLOWING QUESTIONS:
1. According to the author, what is the problem with believing that God has granted a person a piece of land like the West Bank?
2. Where have European Muslims gone to defend their faith, according to the author?
3. How many flashpoints for nuclear conflict does the author say have a strong religious element?

Earlier this year Iran's President Mahmoud Ahmadinejad, speaking to his country's parliament, posed two questions: "Who are our enemies?" and "Why do they hate us?" He described an axis of evil, with Iran's enemies being "all the wicked men of the world, whether abroad or at home". The root cause of their hatred was religious—a loathing of "whomsoever should serve the glory of God". Having described George Bush's atrocities, he told the cheering MPs, "Truly, your great enemy is the American—through that enmity that is in him against all that is of God in you." Fortunately, Iran would not fight alone: it had the support of Muslims around the world. Be bold, he advised, and "you will find that you act for a very great many people that are God's own."

For Mr Ahmadinejad, read Oliver Cromwell; for Iran, England; and for America, Catholic Spain. The quotes above come from a speech made by Cromwell to the English Parliament in 1656. Parliament then passed an oath of loyalty in which English Catholics were asked to disown the pope and most of the canons of Catholic belief, or face losing two-thirds of their worldly goods. Shortly afterwards Cromwell invaded Iran.

"Faith is a source of conflict," reads a sign at St Ethelburga's Centre for Reconciliation and Peace in the City of London—adding that it can also be "a resource to transform conflict". Appropriately, the centre was built in a church blown up in 1993 by Irish terrorists, brought up, no doubt, with tales of Cromwell's atrocities.

Conflict, of course, does not necessarily equate to war. But there are some depressing echoes of Cromwell's time.

Faith is once again prolonging conflict. Religion is seldom the casus belli; indeed, in many struggles, notably the Middle East in modern times, it is amazing how long it took for religion to become a big part of the argument. But once there, it makes conflicts harder to resolve. A squabble over land (which can be divided) or power (which can be shared) or rules (that can be fudged) becomes a dispute over non-negotiable absolutes. If you believe that God granted you the West Bank, or that any form of abortion is murder, compromise is not really possible.

Once again, politicians are stirring up religious passion. Mr Ahmadinejad may not have told Muslims that the Israeli "has an interest in your bowels" (as Cromwell did of Spaniards), but he has called for Israel's removal and denied the Holocaust. Osama bin Laden rages that Islam is under sustained attack: any Muslim who "collaborates" with the West is an apostate.

American leaders have been more careful, but many use religious imagery. In his new book, "God and Gold", Walter Russell Mead compares Ronald Reagan's denunciation of the Godless Soviet Union

O'Farrell, *The Illawary Mercury* (Australia), and PoliticalCartoons.com

(the "Evil Empire") to Cromwell's speech. Franklin Graham spoke for many on the religious right when he denounced Islam as a "very evil and wicked religion". American conservatives seem undecided on whether the battle against "Islamofascism" is the third world war (Newt Gingrich) or the fourth (Norman Podhoretz).

Once again, outsiders are rushing to defend their religions: religious scraps attract money and soldiers. Just as Guy Fawkes, Britain's most famous religious terrorist, hardened his radical beliefs when fighting for Catholicism in the Netherlands, European Muslims have gone to defend their faith in Kashmir, Chechnya and Iraq. Some of the most fervent supporters of India's Hindutva movement come from the diaspora. Many migrants define themselves by their faith, not their new home.

One of the world's great religions, Christianity, split into Catholic and Protestant in the 16th century. Now Islam is having to contend with a sharpening split between Sunni and Shia.

> **FAST FACT**
>
> According to the *New Internationalist*, religious texts have been used to justify executions, cruel and unusual punishment, forced child marriages, and genital mutilation.

Once again nation states are weak: most Middle Eastern countries are recent creations. And there is a ring of instability on Islam's southern frontier, which runs roughly along the 10th parallel from West Africa to the Philippines.

Terrorist outrages are once again presumed to have religious connections, as they would have done in Cromwell's time. In the 1970s terrorism seemed to be the preserve of Maoist guerrillas, middle-class Germans and Italians or the then very secular (and partly Christian-led) Palestine Liberation Organisation. Now three out of the four most likely flashpoints for nuclear conflict—Pakistan-India, Iran and Israel—have a strong religious element. The only exception is North Korea.

Wars Can Be Godless, Too

It is possible that these similarities could escalate into something horrifying. A confrontation between nuclear Iran on one side and Israel and America on the other would reverberate around the globe. But the idea that the world is reverting to a former age is too simplistic.

Most obviously, humanity can find plenty of reasons for genocide and suffering without troubling God. "The 20th century was the most secular and the most bloody in human history," argues George Weigel, a leading American conservative. What he calls "the Godless religions of Nazism and communism" killed tens of millions of people. Each had its theory of salvation, its rites, its prophets, its sacred places and its distinctive idea of morality; but communists and Nazis did not use God to stir up passions. The Cambodian genocide was similarly secular.

Where it does exist, religious conflict is now far less of a top-down affair. No government officially approves of killing people solely because of their religion, and no significant religious leader sanctifies that killing by blessing armadas or preaching crusades. Last year the pope took issue with Islam in a speech at Regensburg, but he also opposed the Iraq war. Most Islamic authorities preach non-violence. Ayatollah Sistani, the most revered Shia on the planet, has often urged restraint in Iraq.

Of course, this does not prevent individual clerics from committing appalling acts of brutality: Catholic priests helped torture people in Argentina, Buddhist monks have led murderous attacks in Sri Lanka and imams have encouraged suicide-bombing in Israel. But every zealot interviewed for this special report, including those with blood near their hands, insisted that his religion was peaceful.

Meanwhile, the power of governments to control religious politics has declined. The wars of religion took place in an age of "cuius regio, eius religio", where the monarch dictated the religion. England once turned to Protestantism because Henry VIII found the Catholic church's rules on matrimony irksome. Nowadays, nobody is trying to improve America's relations with the Middle East by marrying off the Bush twins to Arab princes.

The New Battles

With national armies no longer marching under religious banners, grievances have reappeared in several guises. None of them is easy for the West to deal with. The one that gets most attention is terrorism—especially Islamic terrorism. States are certainly actors in this: Iran may not openly wage religious war, but it has been happy to back Hizbullah in Lebanon and Hamas in Palestine. But then neither Hamas nor Hizbullah is a purely sectarian organisation. Like the IRA in Ireland, they both have political-territorial objectives.

Most of the main jihadist terrorist organisations are bottom-up affairs. Mr bin Laden would no doubt like to control another state (as he once did from Afghanistan). But his organisation has been able to mount attacks and recruit volunteers without help from a government.

The second way in which religion thrusts itself into politics is inter-communal violence. Once again, other forces are often at work, such as tribalism in Nigeria or nationalism in India. But religion supplies the underlying viciousness. Sectarian violence has been responsible for most of the killing in Iraq in the aftermath of the war. Some 68,000 Sri Lankans have died since 1983. Other, lower-level conflicts, such as Catholics and Protestants attacking each other in Mexico's Chiapas, occasionally flare up. Outside parties can play a role in stoking up such struggles (and supplying arms), as Iran has done in Iraq and Syria has done in Lebanon. But most of these fights have a local, tit-for-tat feel. The violence is often set off by events such as marches, feast days or elections.

Third, there is state-based repression, where religion is either the target or the motivation. In the Muslim world the repression is some-times by theocracies (like Iran or Saudi Arabia), against irreligious sorts, such as adulterers, heretics and homosexuals. But it also goes the other way, with secular states (Syria, Egypt, much of North Africa) discriminating against religious dissidents. In the most bizarre exam-ple, China recently banned Buddhist monks in Tibet from reincar-nating without government permission. The religious-affairs agency explained that this was "an important move to institutionalize man-agement of reincarnation". The real purpose is to prevent the Dalai Lama, Tibet's exiled spiritual leader, from being succeeded by some-one from outside China.

Yet the foremost way in which religion has expressed itself around the world has been more peaceful: the ballot box. Religious people have either formed religious parties (such as India's BJP) or con-verted secular ones into more faith-driven outfits (such as America's

Religious strife during the Protestant Reformation brought thirty years of devastation to Europe in the sixteenth century.

Republican Party). In places where religion was frowned upon by the state, such as Mexico or Turkey, greater freedom has allowed the pious to form parties, such as the Catholic-oriented PAN party or the Islamic AK Party.

And it has not just been a case of democracy helping religion. Timothy Shah of the Council on Foreign Relations argues that it can go the other way too. By his calculation, more than 30 of the 80 or so countries that became freer in 1972–2000 owed some of the improvement to religion. Sometimes established churches helped to push for democracy (eg, the Catholic church in Poland), but more often it was pressure from the grassroots: religious people usually look for a degree of freedom (if only to pursue their faith).

All this means that the modern wars of religion are mercifully less violent and all-consuming than their predecessors; but also that tackling the politics of religion is more awkward than it used to be. Culture wars are now global (a subject to which this special report will return).

This complicates foreign policy enormously. Should America focus on the tiny number of angry Muslims with guns, or the millions who have voted for Islamic parties in Egypt, Pakistan, Turkey, Algeria and Palestine? If most religious fanatics were bent on conquest and terror rather than democracy, their causes would be easier to discredit. And if religion were the sole cause of the conflicts, it would be easier to work out "why they hate us".

EVALUATING THE AUTHOR'S ARGUMENTS:

The author of this viewpoint uses several historical examples to support its argument. Which of these examples do you find most effective, and why? Which example do you feel fails to support the magazine's view? Explain your answers using evidence from the text.

Religion Does Not Significantly Contribute to Most Wars

Nick Megoran

"Religion as the primary cause of war is not verifiable from the historical record."

Religion, in particular Christianity, is not a primary cause of war, argues Nick Megoran in the following viewpoint. For one, war has been around much longer than religion, so Megoran reasons religion cannot be war's primary cause. He maintains that while religion has long been linked to violence, the world would not be more peaceful if there were no religions. Rather, Megoran asserts, Christianity and Islam both developed codes of war to ensure that battles were fought for limited reasons, such as self-defense and correcting injustices. He maintains that the Bible is filled with messages of peace and that modern Christians must work to suppress violence.

Megoran is a writer and a lecturer in political geography at Newcastle University in the United Kingdom.

Nick Megoran, "Does Christianity Cause War?" *The Review of Faith & International Affairs,* November 13, 2008. Copyright © 2008 Center on Faith & International Affairs at the Institute for Global Engagement. Reproduced by permission. rfiaonline.org.

AS YOU READ, CONSIDER THE FOLLOWING QUESTIONS:
  1. What does the author say was the earliest cause of war?
  2. What was the purpose of traditions such as "Peace of God" and "Truce of God," according to Megoran?
  3. Who is Søren Kierkegaard, and how does he factor into the author's argument?

T he enduring link between religion and violence is one of the main reasons, in my experience, why people reject Christianity. It is certainly one of the strongest arguments in [atheist and popular science writer] Richard Dawkins' book, *The God Delusion*. Citing various passages of the Bible, he describes the book of Joshua as "a text remarkable for the bloodthirsty massacres it records and the xenophobic [undue fear of foreigners] relish with which it does so." No less an authority than the musician Sir Elton John said religion turns people into "hateful lemmings" and added that he would "ban religion completely."

As a scholar largely preoccupied with the study of war and conflict, I regard the implication of religion in violence as the greatest intellectual challenge to the claim that God exists. Unfortunately, we don't need to search hard to find ample illustrations. The Crusades and the Protestant-Catholic wars of religion in the 16th and 17th centuries are well known. And in numerous European and U.S. wars over the past centuries, Christianity has been invoked by political leaders or participants. It occurs repeatedly in texts and speeches justifying European and American expansion around the world in the 19th and 20th centuries. Jesus commanded Christians to love their enemies—but one would never have guessed as much from the conduct of those claiming to be his followers!

Religion's involvement in historical violence is apparent. However, I do not accept the conclusion that Dawkins and others reach—that the world would be more peaceful if religion in general and, of relevance for this article, Christianity in particular, didn't exist—as following logically from it. . . .

War Predates Major Religions

First, religion as the primary cause of war is not verifiable from the historical record. Warfare, as an organized social practice (as distinct from individual acts of violence), seems to have preceded the development of great world faiths, and to be overwhelmingly the outcome of competition for control of resources. In his summary of the material, respected historian of war John Keegan concludes that the archaeological evidence from Palestine, Egypt, and Mesopotamia shows that the earliest appearances of fixed defensive sites correlate to the first agricultural sites. When hunter-gatherers settled and planted crops, these became a target for other hunter-gatherers, resources that did not exist prior to agriculture. War thus began as a way to secure wealth, the resources of others, and to protect one's own wealth. We know that, for all their talk about civilization, a major rationale for the rise and endurance of European empires in the 19th century was the extraction of wealth from other parts of the world. In our day, many wars are fought over resources. If the main export of Iraq, Kuwait, and Saudi Arabia was dates rather than oil, would the U.S. have invested such heavy military resources in the region over the past two decades?

The author asserts that the twentieth-century Catholic and Protestant conflict was more often about territorial control and constitutional concerns than religious differences.

Religion's Role in Warfare

Religion has not played a major role in most of the wars throughout history. The bolded conflicts are ones in which religious factors played a role in motivating the war, according to the Bradford Peace Studies Group.

Megiddo, First Battle of 1469 B.C.
Zhou defeats the Shang in China ca. 1027 B.C.
Persian Empire Formed 550–530 B.C.
Magahda Wars in India 490–350 B.C.
Greek-Persian Wars 499–488 B.C.
Roman Conquests 498–272 B.C.
Chinese Warring States Period 481–221 B.C.
Peloponnesian War 460–445 B.C.
Great Peloponnesian War 431–404 B.C.
Conquests of Alexander the Great 336–323 B.C.
First Punic War 264–241 B.C.
Second Punic War 218–201 B.C.
Gallic Wars, Campaign of Julius Caesar 58–51 B.C.
Great Roman Civil War 49–44 B.C.
Wars of the Second Triumvirate
Conquests of the Huns 350–453
Arab Conquests 632–732
Crusades 1097–1291
Mongol Conquests 1190–1297
Establishment of the Ottoman Empire 1302–1326
Hundred Years' War 1337–1453
Fall of Constantinople 1453
Italian Wars 1494–1559
Japanese Civil Wars 1560–1584
Moghul Conquest of India 1503–1529
Reformation Wars
Thirty Years' War 1618–1648
Manchu Conquest of China 1618–1650
Spanish Conquests in North and South America
War of Grand Alliance
Great Northern War
War of Austrian Succession
Seven Years' War
War of the American Revolution

Wars of the French Revolution and the Napoleonic Wars 1792–1815
Latin American Wars of Independence 1808–1828
Italian Unification Wars 1848–1866
American Indian Wars
U.S. Civil War 1861–1865
European Colonial Wars Africa, Asia, Pacific 1870–1945
Franco-Prussian War 1870–1871
Russo-Japanese War 1904–1905
Mexican Revolution 1910–1920
World War I
Russian Civil War 1918–1922
Italo-Ethiopian War 1935–1936
Spanish Civil War 1936–1939
World War II
Chinese Civil War 1945–1949
Anticolonial Liberations Wars 1945–1999
Arab-Israeli Wars 1947–1982
U.S.–Soviet Cold War 1948–1991
Korean War 1950–1953
Vietnam War 1961–1975
Northern Ireland 1968–1998
India-Pakistan War Bangladesh 1971
Vietnam-Cambodia War 1978–1989
China-Vietnam War 1979
Afghanistan-USSR War 1979–1989
Iran-Iraq War 1980–1988
Falkland Islands War 1982
Grenada–American Invasion 1983
Panama–American Invasion 1989
Persian Gulf War 1991
Bosnia (1994–1995)
Rwanda-Burundi (1993–1994)
Democratic Republic of Congo Civil War (1994 et seq.)
Chechen Wars (1994 and 1999 to date)
Sudan Civil War (1983 et seq.)
Al Qaeda Terror War (1992 et seq.)
Kosovo (1999)
U.S. and allied invasion of Afghanistan (2001 et seq.)
U.S. and allied invasion of Iraq (2003 et seq.)

Taken from: Greg Austin, Todd Kraneck, and Thom Oommen, *God and War: An Audit and an Explanation*, Bradford Peace Studies Group, 2004.

Today, nationalism—the struggle for the resource of territory that is seen as so vital to a nation—seems to be more important than religion. Academic theologians certainly engage in passionate debate over doctrine. However, "Catholic" and "Protestant" terrorists in Northern Ireland were not fighting over abstract theological and ecclesiastical issues such as the doctrine of grace or the authority of the Pope vis-à-vis church councils; they fought primarily for territory and the constitutional question of whose land is Ulster [a province of Ireland]. Likewise, Al Qaeda's wars appear justified as a global military *jihad* [a holy war waged on behalf of Islam], but in their local manifestations they are often more about patriotic resistance to invasion: Chechens resisting Russians, Iraqis resisting Americans. As [historian and author] Meic Pearse argues, wars are seldom (if at all) mono-causal; religion may be used to justify them, but is rarely the main cause. If religion was suddenly removed from the equation, it is unlikely that the frequency of wars would decrease.

War Would Exist Without Religion

This second atheist assumption—that jettisoning religion would reduce war—is difficult to prove. In fact, religion often serves to suppress wars. [Founder of the Mongol empire] Ghenghis Khan was reported to have said that "The greatest pleasure is to vanquish your enemies and chase them before you, to rob them of their wealth and see those dear to them bathed in tears, to ride their horses and clasp to your bosom their wives and daughters." Religions such as Christianity and Islam developed codes of war that opposed such a spirit, arguing that wars should only be fought in self-defense and to right injustices. Medieval Christian "just war theory" curtailed the right of rulers to make war only in the instance of rectifying an injustice, and imposed limits on the way that war could be fought. It insisted that all who took part had to undertake acts of penance when the war was concluded. In movements like the 11th century "Peace of God" and "Truce of God," certain days of the week, holy festivals, and seasons were identified when warfare was forbidden. The thrust of this tradition was that war was inglorious and undesirable, a last resort to maintain a just order in an imperfect world.

Many theologians at the time did not recognize this limited accommodation to warfare as authentically Christian. Nonetheless, from the earliest times to the Middle Ages, the repeated criticism of Christianity was that it suppressed the ability of people to engage in warfare. In the 2nd century, the pagan writer Celsus complained that widespread adoption of the Christian faith would leave the Roman empire defenseless; in the 16th century Machiavelli bewailed the fact that in his time "most men think more of going to heaven by enduring their injuries than by avenging them," and that "the arts of war" were thus being lost. The existence of modern conventions outlawing certain armaments (like chemical weapons) and practices (such as deliberately attacking civilians, or executing enemy prisoners), however imperfectly applied, are the offspring of a tradition of Christian thought. If religion, and Christianity in particular, had not existed, the martial spirit would have been less suppressed. . . .

Religion Is a Cure for Violence, Not a Cause

Though warfare is associated with Christianity, it has rarely been the main cause of war, and the problematic record of atheism and secularism does not promise a better alternative. But I also want to make the case that Christianity, as it is rightly understood and practiced, is the very essence of peace and the greatest antidote to violence in history. . . .

As I read it, the Bible teaches us that we were made by a God who is "good" and who intends humans to live in relationships with each other. These relationships ought to mirror his character as we live peaceably and unselfishly with each other. However, humanity has clearly not achieved this, and war is perhaps the ugliest and starkest example of such a breakdown in relationships. The theological expression for this at the most general level is "sin". The Biblical narrative is one of God's work in history to restore these relationships. He sent prophets and teachers who provided guidance and moral frameworks, but the climax was sending his son, Jesus, whom, the Bible teaches, lived a (perfect) human life, died on the cross and rose again. He did this to reconcile the world to himself—to take the punishment that the human race deserves for all its wrongdoing, forgive us, and thus re-open the possibility of restored relationships with God and each other, renewing humanity.

The language that the Bible uses so often to describe this is "peace." As the apostle Paul, one of the most important writers of the New Testament and founders of the early church, put it in his letter to the Ephesians, Jesus is "our peace," who made peace by his death on the cross and his resurrection. Paul exhorts the believers to "live at peace with everyone," and calls the Christian message "the Gospel of peace." What did he mean? The foundation of Christianity is that humans can know "peace with God" and be restored to that relationship for which we were created.

This has significant social and political consequences. The Bible asserts that the Church, the body of all believers, is God's visible demonstration of what he has done and is doing. What amazes the apostle Paul in his letters is that the church has broken down social divisions between people—men and women, rich and poor, and in particular national enemies, in his case "Jew and gentile"—and all are united together in Jesus Christ, part of a new, essential, fundamental grouping. Peter calls this a holy nation, an "ethnos," or ethnic group—the church.

Whereas secular nationalism depends upon processes of exclusion and separation, this "holy nation" is open to everyone to join, and those who become its "enemies," who persecute it, are not to be hated and fought, but loved and blessed. Jesus overcame his enemies by his death, defeated them in his dying love for them, and set Christians the same example to follow. . . .

Christians Should Pursue Peace

I began this article by considering historical cases of Christian bellicosity and Dawkins' assertions regarding religion's role in historical violence. The juxtaposition of violent examples with those of Christian peacemaking illustrate the key argument of this article. When the church forgets its call to radical peacemaking, then it "loses its saltiness" and may indeed contribute to violence. But when it remembers it, it can be a remarkably transformative agent for peace.

That is not to say that this is easy. As the sorry histories of atheism and secularism, in both democratic and non-democratic variations, show, humanity's best dreams and hopes can turn horribly sour. Due to its origins and the nature of its authoritative points of reference, Christianity provides more solid and practical resources for suppressing the military spirit in a negative sense, and making peace in a positive one. This claim is not made complacently. As a scholar of conflict, I am painfully aware that the historical intersections of Christianity and violence prevent any glibness. Rather, they should provoke Christians to reflect on the errors made and to explore ways to practice the faith more authentically.

It is not easy to be peacemakers in a world of war, with all the passions it inflames. The 19th century Danish philosopher, Søren Kierkegaard, wrote that Christianity is not hard to understand: "love your enemies" is so simple that even a child can understand it. No, what is difficult, he said, is to put it into practice. The church's historic testimony is that God has equipped Christians—including scholars—for this task, and he has called them to pursue peace in their communities and abroad.

EVALUATING THE AUTHOR'S ARGUMENTS:

Nick Megoran is a lecturer in political geography, a field that studies how geographical factors impact politics, such as how geography can affect voter turnouts. In what ways, if any, do you think his expertise is reflected in this viewpoint?

Chapter 2

When Is War Just?

Explosions in Baghdad mark the beginning of the Iraq War on March 21, 2003. Whether or not the war was justified is the subject of intense debate.

War Is Never Just

Howard Zinn

"Our culture is so war prone that we immediately jump from 'This is a good cause' to 'This deserves a war.'"

In the following viewpoint Howard Zinn argues that a good cause does not justify a war, no matter how just the cause seems. Zinn looks at three wars from American history, the Revolutionary War, the Civil War, and World War II, to make his point. Zinn explains that Canada became independent of England without a war, and not everyone who lived in America benefited from the American Revolution. The Civil War, Zinn claims, was not a simple matter of North versus South or ending slavery. Zinn, who served in World War II, asserts that the war did not defeat fascism, militarism, or racism, and asks what did the fifty million casualties die for? Zinn concludes that some events, such as Hitler invading Czechoslovakia and Poland, seem to have war as the sole course of action, but that is not the case.

Howard Zinn is the author of *A People's History of the United States* and a regular writer for *The Progressive*.

AS YOU READ, CONSIDER THE FOLLOWING QUESTIONS:

1. How did farmers in western Massachusetts drive the British government out without firing a shot a year before the Revolutionary War?

Howard Zinn, "A Just Cause [Not Equal to] a Just War," *The Progressive,* July 2009. Reproduced by permission of The Progressive, 409 East Main Street, Madison, WI 53703. www.progressive.org.

When Is War Just?

2. What class divisions existed in the North and South during the Civil War?

3. According to Zinn, why were the slaves not really freed as a result of the Civil War?

I want to talk about three holy wars. They aren't religious wars, but they're the three wars in American history that are sacrosanct, that you can't say anything bad about: the Revolutionary War, the Civil War, and World War II. Let's look carefully at these three idealized, three romanticized wars. It's important to at least be willing to raise the possibility that you could criticize something that everybody has accepted as uncriticizable.

We're supposed to be thinking people. We're supposed to be able to question everything.

There are things that happen in the world that are bad, and you want to do something about them. You have a just cause. But our culture is so war prone that we immediately jump from "This is a good cause" to "This deserves a war." You need to be very, very comfortable in making that jump.

You might say it was a good cause to get Spain out of Cuba in 1898. Spain was oppressing Cuba. But did that necessarily mean we needed to go to war against Spain? We have to see what it produced. We got Spain out of oppressing Cuba and got ourselves into oppressing Cuba.

You might say that stopping North Korea from invading South Korea was a good idea. The North Koreans shouldn't have done that. It wasn't good. It wasn't right. Does that mean we should have gone to war to stop it? Especially when you consider that two or three million Koreans died in that war? And what did the war accomplish? It started off with a dictatorship in South Korea and a dictatorship in North Korea. And it ended up, after two to three million dead, with a dictatorship in South Korea and a dictatorship in North Korea. I'd be very careful about rushing from one thing to another, from just cause to just war.

Did the Revolutionary War Have to Happen?

The American Revolution—independence from England—was a just cause. Why should the colonists here be oppressed by England? But

The Swiss military on a training
exercise. The Swiss have
maintained their liberty not by
fighting wars, but by making
the conquest of their country
extremely difficult and costly.

therefore, did we have to go to the Revolutionary War? How many people died in the Revolutionary War? Nobody ever knows exactly how many people die in wars, but it's likely that 25,000 to 50,000 people died in this one. So let's take the lower figure—25,000 people died out of a population of three million. That would be equivalent today to two and a half million people dying to get England off our backs. You might consider that worth it, or you might not.

Canada is independent of England, isn't it? Not a bad society. Canadians have good health care. They have a lot of things we don't have. They didn't fight a bloody revolutionary war. Why do we assume that we had to fight a bloody revolutionary war to get rid of England?

In the year before those famous shots were fired, farmers in Western Massachusetts had driven the British government out without firing a single shot. They had assembled by the thousands and thousands around courthouses and colonial offices and they had just taken over and they said goodbye to the British officials. It was a nonviolent revolution that took place. But then came Lexington and Concord, and the revolution became violent, and it was run not by the farmers but by the Founding Fathers. The farmers were rather poor; the Founding Fathers were rather rich.

Who actually gained from that victory over England? It's very important to ask about any policy, and especially about war: Who gained what? And it's very important to notice differences among the various parts of the population. That's one thing we're not accustomed to in this country because we don't think in class terms. We think, "Oh, we all have the same interests." For instance, we think that we all had the same interests in independence from England. We did not have all the same interests.

Do you think the Indians cared about independence from England? No, in fact, the Indians were unhappy that we won independence from England, because England had set a line—in the Proclamation of 1763—that said you couldn't go westward into Indian territory. They didn't do it because they loved the Indians but because they didn't want trouble. When Britain was defeated in the Revolutionary War, that line was eliminated, and now the way was open for the colonists to move westward across the continent, which they did for the next 100 years, committing massacres and making sure that they destroyed Indian civilization.

Did blacks benefit from the American Revolution? Slavery was there before. Slavery was there after. Not only that, we wrote slavery into the Constitution. We legitimized it.

Class Conflict Before and After the Revolution

What about class divisions? Did ordinary white farmers have the same interest in the revolution as a John Hancock or Robert Morris or Madison or Jefferson or the slaveholders or the bondholders? Not really. It was not all the common people getting together to fight against England. The founders had a very hard time assembling an army. They took poor guys and promised them land. They browbeat people and, oh yes, they inspired people with the Declaration of Independence. It's always important, if you want people to go to war, to give them a fine document and have good words: life, liberty, and the pursuit of happiness. Of course, when they wrote the Constitution, they were more concerned with the pursuit of property than the pursuit of happiness. You should take notice of these little things.

We were a class society from the beginning. America started off as a society of rich and poor, people with enormous grants of land and people with no land. And there were bread riots in Boston, and flour riots and rebellions all over the colonies, of poor against rich, of tenants breaking into jails to release people who were in prison for nonpayment of debt. There was class conflict. We try to pretend in this country that we're all one happy family. We're not.

Do you know that there were mutinies in the American Revolutionary Army by the privates against the officers? The officers were getting fine clothes and good food and high pay and the privates had no shoes and bad clothes and they weren't getting paid. They mutinied. Thousands of them. So many in the Pennsylvania line that George Washington got worried, so he made compromises with them. But later when there was a smaller mutiny in the New Jersey line, not with thousands but with hundreds, Washington said execute the leaders, and they were executed by fellow mutineers on the order of their officers. The American Revolution was not a simple affair of all of us against all of them.

Was the Civil War Worth the Cost?

When considering war you need to weigh the human cost against what you gain from war. When you think about the human cost, generally it's an abstraction: 25,000 people died in the Revolutionary War; 600,000 people died in the Civil War; fifty million people died in World War II. But you have to look at that cost not as an abstraction, not as a statistic. You have to look at it as every human being who died, every human being who lost a limb, every human being who came out blind, and every human being who came out mentally damaged. You have to put all of that together when you're assessing that side of the ledger: the cost of the war. Before you ask, "Was it worth it? Was it a just war?" you've got to get that side of the ledger right.

Now, the Civil War was an ugly, brutal war. The 600,000 people who died is equivalent to five million today. Plus, there was amputation after amputation after amputation done in the field without anesthesia. The real human costs were enormous. Who gained?

In the Civil War, we learn about the North versus South, the Blue versus the Gray. But who in the North? Who in the South? What class divisions were there?

Poor white people were conscripted into a war that didn't have much meaning for them. They were being drafted when the rich could get out of the war by paying $300. So there were draft riots in New York and other cities. There was class conflict in the North. There were some people in the North who got rich during the war. J.P. Morgan made a fortune. That's what wars do: They make some people very rich. And it's the poor who go to fight in the wars.

There was class conflict in the Confederacy, too. Most whites were not slaveowners. Maybe one out of six whites was a slaveowner. Poor white soldiers in the South were dying at a much higher rate than the soldiers of the North. As the mayhem went on, as the bloodshed magnified, their families back home were starving because the plantation owners were growing cotton instead of food. And so the wives and the daughters and the girlfriends and the sisters, they began to riot in Georgia and Alabama in protest against the fact that their sons and husbands were dying while the plantation owners were getting rich.

Slaves Were Not Freed by the Civil War

I mustn't ignore the positive side of the Civil War. Yes, emancipation. Freeing the slaves. That's no small matter. You can say maybe the 600,000 dead were worth it if you really freed four million black people and brought them into freedom. But they weren't exactly brought into freedom. They were brought into semi-slavery. They were betrayed by the politicians and the financiers of the North. They were left without resources. They were left at the mercy of the same plantation owners who owned them as slaves and now they were serfs. They couldn't move from one place to another. They were hemmed in by all sorts of restrictions, and many of them were put in jail on false charges. And vagrancy statutes were passed so that employers could pick up blacks off the street and force them to work in a kind of slave labor. So to say that maybe it was OK that 600,000 people died because we ended slavery is not so simple.

Is it possible that slavery could have ended another way, without 600,000 people dead? That's something we don't think of. Just like we don't think of, "Could we have won independence from England without a bloody war?" Remember, there were other countries in the Western Hemisphere that ended slavery without a bloody civil war.

What Did Fifty Million People Die For?

I volunteered to be in World War II and flew bombing missions over Europe. I did it because it was the Good War, it was the right war, it was a just war. After I got out of the war, I began to go back over things and learn about Hiroshima and Nagasaki. When Truman dropped the bomb on Hiroshima, I had just finished my missions in Europe, and was going to go to the Pacific for more missions. So when the war ended soon after Hiroshima, I thought, "Wow, that's great!" I welcomed it. Did I really know what happened when that bomb was dropped on Hiroshima? Did I have any idea what that meant to those hundreds of thousands of people—men, women, and children? No, I did not. When I began to think about it, then I began to think about the people under my bombs. I never saw them. I was flying 30,000 feet above them.

I began to learn something about the reality of Dresden. And I began to learn that three months before Hiroshima and Nagasaki, we sent planes over to firebomb Tokyo, and 100,000 people were killed in one night. Later, when I visited Japan and I visited Hiroshima, I met with survivors of Hiroshima—people without legs and without arms and blind and so on—I began to see what that war meant.

Well, you say, we defeated fascism. Did we, really? Fifty million people dead, and yes, you got rid of Hitler and the Japanese military machine and Mussolini. But did you get rid of fascism in the world? Did you get rid of militarism? Did you get rid of racism? Did you get rid of war? We've had war after war after war. What did those fifty million die for?

Rethinking War

We've got to rethink this question of war and come to the conclusion that war cannot be accepted, no matter what. No matter what the reasons given, or the excuse: liberty, democracy; this, that. War is by definition the indiscriminate killing of huge numbers of people for ends that are uncertain. Think about means and ends, and apply it to war. The means are horrible, certainly. The ends, uncertain. That alone should make you hesitate.

People always ask me, "Yeah, but what else were we to do about this, or that? Independence from England, slavery, Hitler?"

I agree, you had to do something about all these things. But you don't have to do war.

Once a historical event has taken place—Hitler invades Czechoslovakia and Poland, for instance—it becomes very hard to imagine that you could have achieved a result some other way. When something is happening in history, it takes on a certain air of inevitability: This is the only way it could have happened. No.

We are smart in so many ways. Surely, we should be able to understand that in between war and passivity, there are a thousand possibilities.

EVALUATING THE AUTHOR'S ARGUMENTS:

Howard Zinn suggests there were alternatives to war in the Revolutionary War, the Civil War, and World War II. Do you think this suggestion is realistic? Or, were there really no other options besides war in these cases? Explain your reasoning.

Viewpoint
2

War Is Sometimes Just

Amanda Hooper

"A just war is a war that is motivated for the protection of innocent people from tyranny."

Governments are justified in going to war if they do so to protect their citizens, Amanda Hooper claims in the following viewpoint. She argues that governments have the responsibility to fight forces that threaten their citizens with evil and instability. In Hooper's view, war is often a necessary step to establishing peace. It is unrealistic to think war can be avoided, she says, because evil forces that require destruction have always existed and always will. Hooper concludes that war is appropriate when it protects innocent citizens and maintains peace.

At the time this viewpoint was written, Hooper was a student at Bowling Green State University in Bowling Green, Ohio.

AS YOU READ, CONSIDER THE FOLLOWING QUESTIONS:

1. In Hooper's view, why must governments exist?
2. In what way does the author compare government to a babysitter? How does this relate to her argument?
3. What is the meaning of the expression "Epitoma Rei Militaris," as defined by the author?

Amanda Hooper, "War Sometimes Necessary Before Peace Can Be Achieved," *Bowling Green News* (BGNews.com), February 3, 2005. Reproduced by permission of the author.

D oes God say war is a sin? Last week [January 2005] in his column George Valko challenged the "pro-life" Christians with a difficult question. How they can be so adamantly opposed to abortion and yet support a war? Doesn't God say war is a sin? How can these two views ever go hand-in-hand?

War is an armed conflict between nations or factions within a nation. War is the method with which nations are sometimes "forced" to use in order to protect their citizens, but are they committing a sin in the process?

With so many questions, where could we find some answers? Since Christians believe the Bible is the word of God, let's take it from the shelf, dust it off and examine what it says.

The Role of Government Is to Protect Its People from Threats

In Romans 13 in the New Testament, the text clearly says that governments exist to maintain order. "Let every soul be subject to the governing authorities. For there is no authority except from God, and the authorities that exist are appointed by God."

Governments have to exist because there is evil in the world. If all people loved each other unselfishly and worked together instead of for selfish ambition, then governments would not be necessary. Unfortunately, this is not the case.

So, what exactly is the role of the government? Is it to simply make sure our highways are intact, our mail gets where it needs to go and our schools educate children? Well, all of these goals are certainly noble, but the government's ultimate purpose is to protect the people of the nation. This includes maintaining internal order and protecting the borders from out-

FAST FACT

Historians estimate that since the beginning of recorded history (around 3600 B.C.) the Western world has known only about three hundred years of cumulative peace.

side threats as well. "For rulers are not a terror to good works, but to evil. Do you want to be unafraid of the authority? Do what is good, and you will have praise from the same."

Many think that governments have a responsibility to protect their citizens from evil empires, such as Germany under the rule of Adolf Hitler (right), even if it means going to war.

Governments have not only the right, but the responsibility to protect citizens from evil. Evil can not go on ignored and unpunished. "But if you do evil, be afraid; for he does not bear the sword in vain; for he is God's minister, an avenger to execute wrath on him who practices evil."

Governments Can Wage War to Protect Citizens

This means the government has the right to fulfill its purpose as protector by waging war—if necessary.

This is the distinction between individuals aborting babies or murdering one another and governments killing enemies in the midst of war. Individuals are commanded not to murder to fulfill their desires or "needs," but governments are permitted to wage war.

Criteria for a "Just War"

Just War theory has two sets of criteria. The first, *jus ad bellum*, speaks to how a war should be started. The second, *jus in bello*, speaks to how a war should be conducted.

Jus ad bellum (when a war should be waged)

Just cause	War should not be conducted for recapturing things or punishing people. A just war will protect life, fight evil, or defend human rights.
Comparative justice	The injustice suffered by one party must significantly outweigh that suffered by the other.
Legitimate authority	Only legitimate public authorities may start a war.
Right intention	The war must be conducted only for the just reason given for the war, and not for any additional side benefits.
Probability of success	War may not be waged if a cause seems lost.
Last resort	War may not be waged until all peaceful and viable alternatives have been exhausted.
Proportionality	The benefits of the war must equal or outweigh the harm it will cause.

Jus in bello (how war should be conducted)

Distinction	Acts of war must be directed toward enemy combatants only and never civilians.
Proportionality	If civilian injuries are to be sustained, these must be in proportion to the value of the military target and not in excess of it.
Military necessity	A just war will keep use of force to a minimum.

Taken from: Compiled by the editor.

Imagine that you are hired by a family to baby-sit for their children. Your role and responsibility is to watch and protect the children. Now imagine a large dog suddenly runs over and intends to harm the children in your care. It is not only your right, but job to do whatever you must do to protect the children. Now, if those same children were to wander over to a friendly, harmless dog and start kicking it or throwing stones at it, your job and responsibility would be to stop the kids and discipline them for acting foolishly according to their own desires. Governments have a different role than citizens, just as the baby-sitter has a different responsibility than the kids.

Times of war pervade history. In fact, war is the common theme in humanity. This is because although times change, human nature does not. Evil existed in ancient Babylon, as it did in Nazi Germany, as it does today in many places throughout the world. History is often measured in the time and duration of wars.

Clearly, when a nation commits to war, it is a grave decision. A just war is a war that is motivated for the protection of innocent people from tyranny. A leader who commits his country to war bears the huge responsibility of being accountable for the motives of war. Power can be a burden it seems.

War Is Sometimes Necessary for Peace to Occur

Sometime issues that look like opposites really are not. Is war the opposite of peace?

There is an ancient Roman expression "Epitoma Rei Militaris," which means "If you want peace, prepare for war." Sometimes a season of war must be endured to establish peace. Ideally, that season would never exist, or be short instead of a long winter of discontent and suffering. But, when winter ends, we can be grateful for the hope and peace spring brings.

> ### EVALUATING THE AUTHOR'S ARGUMENTS:
>
> Hooper says that war is necessary to achieve peace. What do you think of this claim? Does it sound true or like a contradiction? Explain your reasoning.

Viewpoint 3

The Iraq War Is Just

Douglas Stone

"We had to go to war [in Iraq], because the only sure way to ensure our national security is to drain the swamp of terrorism."

In the following viewpoint Douglas Stone argues that the United States was justified in its decision to go to war against Iraq. He thinks the Iraq War was the best way to put a stop to Islamic terrorism. According to Stone, war was necessary because Arab countries refused to stop terrorism on their own. Furthermore, in Stone's opinion, the Iraq War was not necessarily bad for that country—he says it could help Iraq become an open, free, and democratic society, one that other Arab nations can emulate. He concludes that even though mistakes have been made during the war, the war itself was the right action for the right cause.

Stone is a senior fellow with the Center for Security Policy, an organization that works to develop successful national security policies.

AS YOU READ, CONSIDER THE FOLLOWING QUESTIONS:
1. What was the primary reason that the United States went to war in Iraq, according to the author?
2. In Stone's view, what reality about war do adults normally understand?
3. What does the phrase "paper tiger" mean in the context of the viewpoint?

It needs to be said: It was smart to go to war in Iraq; it was courageous to go to war; but most of all—even though there are few things as horrific as war—it was necessary to go to war against Iraq. Had we not gone to war against Iraq in 2003, we almost certainly would have done so there or in another Arab country at another time, and all in less advantageous circumstances. Iraq was the right time, right place, right war.

We had to go to war, because the only sure way to ensure our national security is to drain the swamp of terrorism: to finally begin the process of wrenching the Arab world from a culture of backwardness, oppression and hatred toward the West.

And as the war seems finally to show some hope of success, it isn't time to leave. We need to finish the job as we remind ourselves why we are there.

We Had Good Reasons to Go to War

Too many forget that there was massive support for the war in 2003: from left to right, Democrats and Republicans; and if many of our European allies did not support going to war in early 2003, their intelligence services were supporting the views of our own multi-agency analyses: that Saddam had WMDs [weapons of mass destruction], a belief [Iraqi president] Saddam [Hussein] almost undoubtedly nurtured in order to overawe his Iranian neighbors.

WMDs were the primary reason we went to war. Others include Saddam's genocidal campaign against the Kurds and his infringement of the no-fly zone, which violated the armistice that had halted the fighting in 1991 [the Gulf War] and gave the powers opposing him the legal right under international law to resume hostilities.

In fact, there is reason to believe that even if [Al] Gore had been elected President in 2000 that we would have gone to war; perhaps a bit later, after an additional UN resolution or two, but at some point we would have done so.

And so the war came.

War Is Always Difficult

Came with all its brutality and horror and mistakes, most notably in the occupation. But that's no reason now to decry our involvement.

Success in Iraq

Both attacks and troop deaths have declined since more troops were sent to Iraq in 2007. Supporters of the war argue the war was fought for just causes and is capable of being won.

Overall Iraq Attack Trends

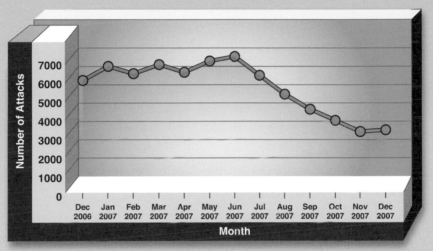

Note: Graph includes potential attacks (IEDs/mines found and cleared) and executed attacks.

Coalition Killed in Action

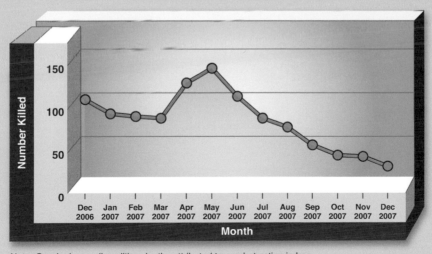

Note: Graph shows all coalition deaths attributed to combat action in Iraq.

It's easy to favorably compare "what might have been" but the reality is that all wars are filled with unpleasant surprises.

Adults normally understand and accept that—as they accepted during the Civil War such setbacks as Fredericksburg [where Union armies suffered great losses] or during World War II the disaster of Kasserine Pass [the first large-scale battle of American and German forces where the American troops suffered many casualties] or the horrific early losses in our early daylight strategic bombing campaign.

No matter how the occupation was handled, there would have been difficulties. There's no way of telling whether other choices would have been better than the choices that were made. The great advantage of the choices we didn't make is that they exist as pristine "what ifs," unsullied by reality.

Arab Nations Would Not Stop Terrorism

The reality is that Saddam would have had to have been removed at some point, and the decrepit state he held together by terror was

Former U.S. secretary of state Colin Powell holds a vial he once thought indicated Iraq was manufacturing anthrax and other weapons of mass destruction. The author says that although the war unearthed no WMDs, it was still justified.

bound to blow apart. Better sooner than later to get a head start on taking on a country at the heart of the Arab world and Arab mythology that had been fomenting terrorism, oppressing its people and otherwise helping to sustain a collective Arab culture that is a petri dish for terrorism.

We have urged our Arab "friends" to make changes that would discourage terrorism. We've cajoled, pressed, implored and begged them. We've bribed, demanded and threatened. But nothing worked. We finally had to take the most vile offender by the scruff of its neck and force it to change.

FAST FACT

According to the Documental Centre for Human Rights in Iraq, more than 600,000 civilians were killed under the regime of Saddam Hussein, who was overthrown by U.S. forces in March 2003.

Iraq Is Making Progress

Contemporary Iraq is not a paradise; even our best hopes for it remain far short of what we in the West would regard as a humane, tolerant and decent society. But there seems to be progress toward that goal, and more than any Arab country today Iraq has a chance to create a pluralistic society that does not oppress its people, that offers hope for the future and that opposes terrorism; and in becoming this kind of state offers a model to the rest of the Arab world.

Having taken on Saddam in 2000, we have five years of experience in counterinsurgency in the center of the Arab world, and we're five years closer to winning the War for the Free World in the only way possible: by changing the culture that allows terrorism to survive and flourish.

Had we waited, the war would have been more difficult and the stakes much greater.

Leaving Iraq Would Not Lead to Real Peace

Now that things seem to be moving in the right direction is not the time to pull out according to an artificial time table driven not only by ignorance of the facts on the ground but the exigencies of party politics.

Now is the time to reap the benefits of the sacrifice of money, national prestige and most important of all, the lives of some of our best young people. It is not the time to retreat and reveal to all and sundry that we are a paper tiger.

Those who support surrender say that there would be peace. And there would be peace. But a counterfeit peace: the fallacy of the false alternative: peace for a week, a month, a year, but what of two or ten or fifty years, the world of our children and grandchildren?

To leave without victory would be to return to the beginning, and we would have to do it all over again in a few years. Understood or not, it was the world's good fortune that we were able to take on Saddam when we did: It was the right time, right place, right war.

That's why we fight.

EVALUATING THE AUTHOR'S ARGUMENTS:

One of the key arguments in Douglas Stone's viewpoint is that weapons of mass destruction (WMDs) were a main reason the United States went to war in Iraq. But no WMDs were ever found in that country. Given this fact, do you think including this casus belli (a justification for war) in his argument weakens it? Why or why not?

The Iraq War Is Not Just

Robert W. McElroy

> *"Scrutiny of the current situation in Iraq reveals that four of the required foundations for the moral use of force are not currently being met."*

The war in Iraq is unjust because it fails to meet four key criteria, Robert W. McElroy argues in the following viewpoint. According to McElroy, war is moral only if it is based on a just cause, is for the right intention, is a last resort, and is fought with a reasonable hope for success. In McElroy's view, the Iraq war meets none of these standards. In his opinion, the United States had no reason to go to war in that country: Doing so has hurt both the United States and Iraq. Furthermore, the United States did not exhaust diplomacy before waging war and will most likely lose there. Therefore, McElroy believes the United States must withdraw its troops from Iraq immediately and refrain from entering other unjust wars in the future.

McElroy is a pastor and the author of *Morality and American Foreign Policy: The Role of Ethics in International Affairs.*

AS YOU READ, CONSIDER THE FOLLOWING QUESTIONS:

1. Why does McElroy think democratizing Iraq is not a just cause for war?

Robert W. McElroy, "Why We Must Withdraw from Iraq: An Argument from Catholic Just-War Principles," *America Magazine,* vol. 196, April 30, 2007, pp. 10–15. Copyright 2007 www.america magazine.org. All rights reserved. Reproduced by permission of America Press. For subscription information, visit www.americamagazine.org.

2. In the author's opinion, what action by the Bush administration was testimony to its reluctance to view war in Iraq as a last resort?
3. What does the author say is the "only moral warrant" remaining for U.S. troops in Iraq?

O ne implication of [the] strong presumption against war in Catholic moral teaching is that moral scrutiny of the decision to wage war should take place not merely at the beginning of a conflict, but at every stage of its duration. If it is morally required by just-war thinking that there be a just cause, approval by competent authority, the presence of right intention, reasonable hope of success and proportionality of means in any initial decision to wage war, is it not also morally required that these conditions be present throughout the conflict if war is to be continued? The moral warrant for war can hardly be said to continue if the foundations for that warrant have disappeared.

The Iraq War Has No Just Cause

Scrutiny of the current situation in Iraq reveals that four of the required foundations for the moral use of force are not currently being met.

1. *Just Cause.* The most troubling element of the argument that the United States has had a continuing just cause in waging war in Iraq is that the nature of that just cause has constantly shifted during the past four years of war. Originally it was proposed that the possession of massive stores of chemical and biological weapons by the regime of Saddam Hussein, an aggressive and brutal expansionist dictator, clearly satisfied the demand that war could be waged morally in order to repel legitimately anticipated aggression. Then, when weapons of mass destruction were not found, it was proposed that the war was just because Saddam Hussein was committing aggression against his own people and neighbors. Then, after Saddam was arrested, the case for a continuing just cause has come to rest upon America's desire to transform Iraq into a stable democracy.

But transformational democratization falls outside the criteria of the just cause as it has been formulated in the modern age. Because of the destructiveness of modern warfare, only the repulsion of aggression is now viewed as an acceptable cause to go to war, not the desire to transform other societies. This defect in the theory of transformation is magnified by the fact that the justice of America's cause must now be measured not by the abstract dream of democratization but by the concrete role that the United States has undertaken in Iraq: the defense of an unstable government of questionable commitment to equal justice in an environment where centrifugal regional, ethnic and religious forces threaten to tear the nation apart.

Former president George W. Bush meets with Lee Hamilton, left, and James Baker, right, both members of the Iraq Study Group. The author criticizes Bush's reluctance to accept the group's diplomatic recommendations.

The Iraq War Lacks Right Intention

2. *Right Intention.* As America evaluates its commitment to remain in Iraq, the criterion of right intention presents an ever greater obstacle to those who advocate sustained military occupation. For right intention demands that a nation wage war only to address the specific grave wrong that led to war. Increasingly in the national debate on Iraq, the justification for continuing the use of military force is not peace and stability in Iraq, but the necessity of demonstrating America's continuing commitment to fight terrorism in the world. The notion that a defeat in Iraq will severely damage the United States' reputation in the world is taking center stage in this nation's domestic debate, and in the process America's fulfillment of the just-war requirement of a right intention is evaporating. Considerations of reputation can never fulfill the criterion of right intention, and insofar as they forge the United States' decisions and commitment in Iraq, they render continued military occupation there morally illegitimate.

War Was Not Necessary

3. *Last Resort.* The world was dubious that the United States had exhausted all diplomatic options for peace when it went to war against Iraq in 2003, and the world should be dubious that it is exhausting those options now. The refusal of the [George W.] Bush administration to accept the recommendation of the Baker-Hamilton commission (The Iraq Study Group) that America should begin a direct and sustained dialogue with Iran and Syria in the pursuit of peace in Iraq is a testimony to the Bush administration's continuing reluctance to treat military action as a last resort. If Catholic theology carries with it a strong presumption against war, it also carries with it the implication that the use of force, unaccompanied by a constant, sustained and strenuous search for viable peaceful alternatives, is never legitimate.

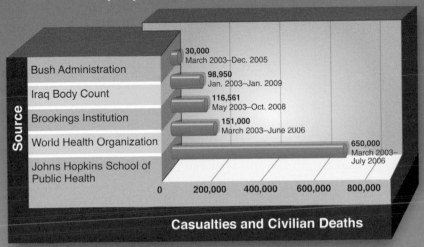

Iraqi Casualties Since the Start of War

Thousands of Iraqis have been killed in the Iraq War, which some believe was unjustly started.

Source	Casualties and Civilian Deaths
Bush Administration	30,000 — March 2003–Dec. 2005
Iraq Body Count	98,950 — Jan. 2003–Jan. 2009
Brookings Institution	116,561 — May 2003–Oct. 2008
World Health Organization	151,000 — March 2003–June 2006
Johns Hopkins School of Public Health	650,000 — March 2003–July 2006

Scale: 0, 200,000, 400,000, 600,000, 800,000

Note: Neither the United States nor the Iraq governments provide an official count of Iraqi civilian deaths. Estimates and time periods measured from other sources vary widely.

Taken from: National Public Radio, February 23, 2009.

4. *Reasonable Hope of Success.* The level of tragedy in the United States' intervention in Iraq becomes apparent when one recognizes that the greatest difficulty of assessing this criterion lies not in measuring the level of well-founded hope for the American cause in Iraq, but in defining what constitutes success. Each milestone of limited success—the fall of Baghdad, the establishment of a new government and the writing of a constitution—has been followed by a deterioration of the situation in the country as a whole. As a consequence, the United States is now unwilling to establish public milestones and to define achievable success in any concrete way.

Iraq Does Not Meet Criteria for Just War

The original moral warrant for the intervention in Iraq has collapsed along with the American dreams of a swift and relatively peaceful democratization of Iraqi society. Any just-war argument that a new moral warrant has emerged founders upon the difficulty of demonstrating that the current situation meets the tests of just cause, right intention, last resort and reasonable hope for success.

Catholic advocates for continued military occupation in Iraq on just-war grounds have turned to the one criterion of the just-war tradition whose importance and even epistemological [a branch of philosophy devoted to investigating the origin, nature, methods, and limits of human knowledge] possibility they had previously questioned at every stage of the decision to go to war: the criterion of proportionality. In the months leading up to the war and in the first years of the intervention in Iraq, advocates argued that the complexities of war and geopolitics in the modern age made it impossible to predict with any precision whether the evils unleashed by war in Iraq would outweigh the good to be accomplished by war. They proposed that epistemic modesty [that one's opinions should not extend beyond experience] is required in any moral analysis of the contingencies of war and rejected as speculative and unfounded the many arguments of specialists in the Middle East who predicted that intervention in Iraq would produce evils greater than the good likely to be achieved.

Now these same advocates of continued American military occupation in Iraq propose that this epistemic modesty is to be cast aside, and that the one certainty in Iraq is that American withdrawal would be a catastrophic blow to peace and just order in the world. In other words, just-war advocates are asserting that they can in fact analyze the consequences of remaining in Iraq versus those of withdrawal, and can know those comparative consequences in sufficient detail to ground a moral mandate to continue military action in Iraq.

It must be emphasized that these advocates for continued American military occupation in Iraq proceed from a profound moral concern that U.S. actions in Iraq have created moral obligations for the United States that can be satisfied only by achieving a peaceful, secure Iraq. When one views the history of brutality and repression that has been visited upon Iraq by a succession of imperialist powers and homegrown dictators, one cannot help but be drawn to such a hope. But hope is not reality, and neither hope nor a sense of moral obligation is sufficient to ground a moral mandate for war in just-war thinking. . . .

We Must Withdraw from Iraq

In a . . . twist of politics, the burden of proof in the current debate about U.S. withdrawal from Iraq is being placed upon those who advocate withdrawal; they must prove that withdrawal will not destabilize Iraq. In Catholic thinking, the calculus is just the opposite. Those advocating continued military action in Iraq face the burden of proof not only to demonstrate that remaining in Iraq is clearly more likely to yield more good than evil, but also to show that such continued action meets the conditions imposed by just-war thinking. Facing the current realities in Iraq, this burden is impossible to meet. The only moral warrant that emerges from any effort to apply rigorous just-war thinking to Iraq is the warrant to move immediately toward a measured and prudently crafted American military withdrawal.

EVALUATING THE AUTHOR'S ARGUMENTS:

In the viewpoint you just read, Robert McElroy uses history, facts, and examples to make his argument that the war in Iraq was not just. He does not, however, use any quotations to support his point. If you were to rewrite this article and insert quotations, what authorities might you quote from? Where would you place these quotations to bolster the points McElroy makes?

Viewpoint

5

The War on Terror Is Necessary

Rudolph W. Giuliani

"Every American understands that homeland security is at the heart of a president's responsibility."

It is just for America to conduct the war on terrorism because doing so protects the United States, its borders, and the economy, Rudolph W. Giuliani asserts in the following viewpoint. He contends that in order for the U.S. government to effectively combat terrorism, it must help the intelligence community share information with law enforcement agencies. To do this, he recommends developing a computerized counterterrorism program and putting a stop to illegal immigration. According to Giuliani, these steps will make America more secure and help it defeat Islamic extremism. He concludes that any efforts to protect Americans from terrorist attacks are just and necessary.

Giuliani served as mayor of New York City from 1994 to 2001.

AS YOU READ, CONSIDER THE FOLLOWING QUESTIONS:

1. What three principles should homeland security be based on, according to Guiliani?

Rudolph W. Giuliani, "The Resilient Society: A Blueprint for Homeland Security," *City Journal,* vol. 18, Winter 2008. Copyright The Manhattan Institute. Reproduced by permission.

2. According to the author, what 1978 act must be modernized and expanded to address new technologies?
3. Why does the author say that the story of Ra'ed al-Banna shows the connection between homeland security and border security?

I n the first decade of the twenty-first century, the United States has confronted both the deadliest attack and one of the most destructive natural disasters in the nation's history. The term "homeland security" wasn't part of the national debate during the 2000 election. Now, after September 11 and Hurricane Katrina, every American understands that homeland security is at the heart of a president's responsibility.

There have been no fewer than 14 attempted domestic terrorist attacks and nine international plots against American citizens and interests since 9/11, according to reports in the public record. There have been plots to blow up the Brooklyn Bridge and airplanes crossing the Atlantic. Terrorists have conspired to murder American soldiers at Fort Dix and planned to ignite the fuel lines beneath John F. Kennedy International Airport. Not a single post-9/11 plot on U.S. soil has succeeded to date. That is no accident; it is a measure of our increased vigilance as a nation.

Fighting Terrorists Is an Ongoing Challenge

The fight against al-Qaida and other terrorist groups will be America's central challenge for years to come. We will achieve victory in what I call the Terrorists' War on Us only by staying on offense: defeating terrorist organizations and hunting down their leaders, wherever they are; helping Afghanistan and Iraq establish stable and representative governments; aiding the spread of good governance throughout the Muslim world; and defeating militant Islam in the war of ideas.

Such international efforts are essential to winning this war, but not sufficient. We must also protect our people and economy, secure our borders, and prevent terrorist attacks here at home. These responsibilities are the domestic dimension of the larger struggle, and they require a focus on more than terrorism. As Stephen Flynn points out in his book *The Edge of Disaster*, "Nearly 90 percent of Americans are

The War on Terror Has Been Just

Americans believe that the War on Terror is among the most positive contributions the United States has recently made to the world.

"In your opinion, would you say that the United States tends to play a positive role, a negative role, or neither a positive nor a negative role in the following?"

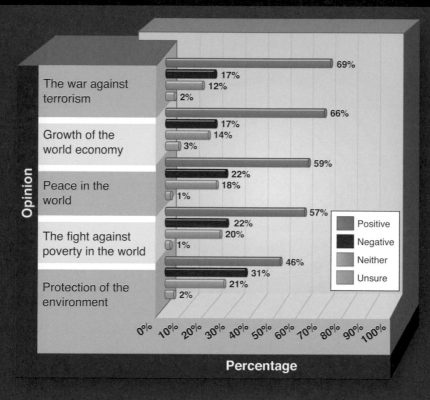

Taken from: The Gallup Poll, May 21–23, 2004.

currently living in locations that place them at moderate to high risks of earthquakes, volcanoes, wildfires, hurricanes, flooding, or high-wind damage." Preparing for terrorist attacks and for natural disasters are complementary goals: when cities and states prepare for natural disaster, they also strengthen our response to potential terrorism.

The [Barack Obama] administration's approach to homeland security should be based on three core principles: prevention, preparedness, and resilience.

Preventing Terrorism Is Our Number One Priority

Preventing terrorist attacks before they happen must be our primary goal. Of course, America must stay on offense internationally when it comes to WMDs [weapons of mass destruction], using determined diplomacy and economic measures to discourage states from trading in dangerous materials that threaten Americans. Nations that continue in the trade must face the seizure of shipments—or worse. Here at home and at ports overseas, we must deploy state-of-the-art radiation detection technology to shield against nuclear fissile material, dirty bombs, and other radiological weapons, and we must proceed with the development and stockpiling of vaccines as a defense against bioterror. We also need to be ready for other forms of attack, such as cyberterrorism—a weapon of mass disruption. Digital technologies drive our nation's economy and control much of our critical infrastructure. America cannot afford to wait for a digital Pearl Harbor before we begin taking the cyberterrorism threat seriously.

But these steps, as important as they are, will not solve the now widely recognized problem of getting our federal intelligence and law enforcement officers to share information so that they can "connect the dots" to uncover terrorist attacks before they happen. Some people theorize, based on the 9/11 Commission report, that the attacks of September 11 might have been prevented if the CIA and FBI had overcome the institutional barriers between and within the agencies and shared information. To take just one well-known example, the CIA knew in early 2000 that one suspected al-Qaida terrorist had acquired a U.S. visa and that another had flown to California. But Langley didn't tell the FBI or register the men with the State Department's watch list. As a result, two future 9/11 hijackers slipped into the U.S. Whether communication would or would not have been enough to lead to actions to prevent the attacks, it certainly is prudent to make sure this gap is closed in the future.

Roadblocks to Gathering Information

Several kinds of barriers hampered us in the 1990s. Some reflected the cultural differences between prosecution-oriented law enforcement agencies and the intelligence community's preference for information collection. Others were legally required, such as the restrictions on sharing information derived through grand juries and criminal wiretaps. Still others were self-imposed, such as the infamous "wall" erected by the Clinton justice department in 1995, which complicated collaboration between the FBI's foreign counterintelligence agents and its criminal investigators.

Such "stovepiping" of information must not continue. We need to build on the [George W.] Bush administration's efforts, such as the USA Patriot Act, to break down the barriers among federal agencies and between foreign and domestic intelligence. The Patriot Act removed barriers to information sharing between the intelligence community and law enforcement, but there is still more to do. We must guard against the danger that the newly created Office of the Director of National Intelligence will become just another layer of bureaucracy that impedes the information flow rather than facilitates it. And we need to pay close attention to unsettling lower-court decisions that raise the specter of the wall's reemergence, and to the weakening of the Patriot Act by judicial fiat.

The Foreign Intelligence Surveillance Act, enacted in 1978 to exclude eavesdropping on foreign communications from judicial oversight, must be modernized and expanded to encompass not just phones, as the current law does, but also newer technologies, such as the fax machine and the Internet. Antiquated laws—enacted when such technologies weren't part of everyday life—cannot be allowed to hamstring our federal law enforcement and foreign intelligence services. Some members of Congress want to throw as many legal obstacles as possible in front of FBI agents and intelligence officers as they try to intercept communications between known al-Qaida leaders and U.S.-based operatives who will carry out attacks. This is the last thing we should do.

New Technology Can Help

Getting and keeping federal agencies communicating with one another isn't enough. An effective homeland security plan also has to establish links to, and make use of, the valuable information collected by the country's 800,000 state and local law enforcement officers. We should view these officers as counterterrorism resources—"first preventers," as the Manhattan Institute's R. P. Eddy calls them. Even beyond uniformed services, people such as DMV [Department of Motor Vehicles] clerks, and even everyday citizens, may notice clues that would help law enforcement identify would-be terrorists. It was a clerk at Circuit City, after all, who provided the key tip that enabled federal authorities to stop the Fort Dix plot.[1] . . .

To gather and analyze such useful information, first preventers can be assisted by the widespread implementation of a "Terrorstat" program, an idea proposed by former NYPD commissioner William Bratton and criminologist George Kelling. Terrorstat would build on the proven principles of Compstat, the computerized crimemapping system devel-

FAST FACT

In 2008, according to the U.S. State Department, 11,770 terrorist attacks occurred worldwide, resulting in the deaths of 15,765 people.

oped by the New York Police Department in the 1990s and now used by police departments nationwide. By bringing all crime and arrest data together by category and by neighborhood, Compstat revolutionized policing, enabling officers to focus their efforts in problem areas, armed with up-to-the-minute, accurate intelligence, rapid deployment of resources, individual accountability, and relentless follow-up. Terrorstat would do the same for counterterrorism.

Beating Terrorists at Their Own Game

Terrorstat would not only capture information about terrorism-related arrests and distribute it to law enforcement officials; it would also fuse that information with data on arrests for crimes that on the surface seem unrelated to terrorism but may prove to be precursors to an attack. The investigation of the ordinary can help prevent the extraordinary.

Terrorists prepare for their activities with preattack surveillance and finance them with ordinary criminal actions. Consider a 2005 plot in which a jihadist cell aimed to unleash a wave of violence in Southern California. One of the conspirators made the mistake of dropping his cell phone during what appeared to be a straightforward gas-station

1. A 2007 plan by six Islamic terrorists to attack a New Jersey military base.

robbery in Torrance, California. Local police drew information from the phone that set off an FBI-led investigation that eventually unraveled the plot. Or consider the case of Dhiren Barot, a now-imprisoned al-Qaida operative who developed detailed pre-attack surveillance reports before 9/11 on major financial buildings in Washington, D.C., New York, and New Jersey. None of the security guards at any of the facilities that he cased, including the World Bank, the New York Stock Exchange, and the Prudential building in Newark, detected him. He was captured only after the CIA raided a terrorist safe house in Pakistan in 2004 and found Barot's casing reports on a computer.

The Department of Homeland Security, in coordination with state homeland security offices, should train public and private security personnel around the nation to recognize and report terrorist pre-attack activity. Terrorstat would provide a simple, structured, and consistent way for security personnel to report information to a larger intelligence network, including the National Counterterrorism Center—leading to investigations that can disrupt terrorist plots before they result in deadly attacks.

Our Borders Must Be More Secure

Homeland security and border security are inseparable in the twenty-first century. The story of Ra'ed al-Banna is a chilling reminder of why. On June 14, 2003, al-Banna was denied entry into the U.S. at Chicago's O'Hare International Airport by Customs and Border Protection inspectors, who questioned him after their Automated Targeting System identified him as warranting further scrutiny. On February 28, 2005, al-Banna blew up himself and at least 125 others outside a health clinic in Hilla, Iraq. It was one of the deadliest suicide bombings committed by al-Qaida in Iraq. We'll never know if al-Banna was coming to the U.S. to inflict similar harm, but strong border security prevented him from having the opportunity.

Still, a recent National Intelligence Estimate concluded that al-Qaida is intensifying its efforts to place operatives within the United States. Security must improve at official ports of entry like O'Hare, as well as along our porous land borders. Ending illegal immigration and identifying every noncitizen in the nation are crucial to preventing terror. We need a tamperproof biometric ID card for all noncitizens

Rudolph Giuliani, the author of this viewpoint, believes the war on terrorism is a just, noble, and necessary effort that keeps the United States and its allies safe.

and a single national database of noncitizens in our country that would include information about when they are required to leave. And if noncitizens commit crimes, they should be deported after serving their time.

To bring real order to the border, we should establish a "Borderstat" program, also based on Compstat principles. Borderstat would use technology to monitor illegal border crossings and compare them with captures. It would enable us to hold field commanders—including border patrol sector chiefs and Immigration and Customs Enforcement special agents in charge—accountable for what goes on in their areas. The successful completion of the Secure Border Initiative (SBI), ongoing since 2006—which promises to help us gain control of the borders through the construction of both physical and virtual technological fences—will be an essential step in this effort. . . .

Though we must make America more secure, we must also show our friends around the world that America is a country open for business, not a closed-door fortress. The best and the brightest should come to America—to study here, to work here, and in some cases to become American citizens. It is only through this process that we will deepen the connections between America and the Islamic world that will prove essential in prevailing over radical Islamic extremism.

EVALUATING THE AUTHOR'S ARGUMENTS:

Rudolph W. Giuliani was the mayor of New York City during the September 11, 2001, attacks. Earlier in his career, he served as associate attorney general in Ronald Reagan's administration. In what ways do you think that his opinions about terrorism have been affected by these experiences? Do you think his arguments are more or less compelling because of his background? Explain your answers.

The War on Terror Is A Mistake

H.D.S. Greenway

"The problem with declaring a war on terrorism is that terrorism is a tactic, and terror an emotion. They cannot be defeated."

The George W. Bush administration's "war on terror" was a mistake, H.D.S. Greenway asserts in the following viewpoint. According to Greenway, one cannot make war on terror or terrorists because terror is an emotion, and terrorists an easily renewable resource—when one is destroyed, another can usually be recruited. He suggests that terrorists be treated like criminals rather than as military combatants, which wrongly glorifies their position. Furthermore, as part of the war on terror, he argues that the United States has curbed civil liberties and detained innocent people, both of which are unjust, in his opinion. Greenway says terrorism succeeds when it divides countries and threatens civil liberties. Therefore, the United States and its allies should champion democracy and the rule of law if they really want to defeat terrorists.

Greenway is a columnist and the former editorial page editor for the *Boston Globe*.

H.D.S. Greenway, "War Is Not the Right Weapon," GlobalPost.com, February 16, 2009. Copyrighted © 2009 by Global News Enterprises, LLC. Reproduced by permission.

AS YOU READ, CONSIDER THE FOLLOWING QUESTIONS:
1. According to General David Petraeus, what problems can the United States not kill its way out of?
2. What, according to Greenway, was "the mother of all over-reactions"?
3. What can be accomplished if terrorist attacks can be kept in perspective, according to Louise Richardson?

Almost every expert on terrorism that I have ever met believes that the [George W.] Bush administration's terminology, "war on terrorism" or the "global war on terror," was a mistake. Louise Richardson, late of Harvard and now principal of St. Andrews University, put it well when she wrote: "We cannot defeat terrorism by smashing every terrorist movement. And efforts to do so will only generate more terrorists, as has happened repeatedly in the past. We should never have declared a global war on terrorism, knowing that such a war can never be won."

Or as Gen. David Petraeus has said, we cannot kill our way out of the problems of insurgency and civil strife.

One Cannot Make "War" Against "Terror"

The problem with declaring a war on terrorism is that terrorism is a tactic, and terror an emotion. They cannot be defeated. They can be overcome. They can be ameliorated, contained, but never defeated. To declare war on them is setting a goal that can never be realized, and is therefore self-defeating.

The call to war implies that force is the only tool that can be used. Combating Islamic terrorist groups may require force from time to time, but, far more will depend on good police work and luck. "Our objective should not be the unattainable goal of obliterating terrorism," Richardson writes, "rather we should pursue the more modest and attainable goal of containing terrorist recruitment and constraining resort to the tactic of terrorism."

The United States Has Responded Poorly to Terrorism

Traveling around Europe these days one finds that our allies have become more and more disenchanted with "war on terror." British

Foreign Secretary, David Miliband, wrote an article in *The Guardian* last month [in January 2009] that sounded like a personal plea to President Barack Obama. He admitted that the term "had some merit: it captured the gravity of the threats, the need for solidarity, and the need to respond urgently, where necessary, with force."

Taliban and al Qaeda detainees at the U.S. naval base in Guantanamo Bay. The author says that terrorism is a tactic that cannot be defeated by conventional warfare.

© 2009 Dave Granlund, PoliticalCartoons.com

"But ultimately," the foreign minister wrote, "the notion is misleading and mistaken." He continued: "We should respond to terrorism by championing the rule of law, not subordinating it, for it is the cornerstone of the democratic society. We must uphold our commitments to human rights and civil liberties at home and abroad. That is surely the lesson of Guantanamo."

And: "Terrorists succeed when they render countries fearful and vindictive; when they sow division and animosity; when they force countries to respond with violence and repression. The best response is to refuse to be cowed."

As Richardson has pointed out, declaring war on a terrorist organization is to give it too much glory and prestige, which is what it seeks.

Terrorists Should Be Treated Like Criminals

In France, a senior official involved in anti-terrorism told me that wherever possible, it is better to avoid exceptional laws for the investigations and the trial of terrorist cases. "Even if a strict common law application isn't adapted for terrorist affairs, French law provides rules that are essentially the same as those used for organized crime."

Better to treat terrorist organizations as you would criminal conspiracies than to elevate them to the status of war combatants. Giving terrorists such lofty prestige is to give them an invaluable recruiting tool. "Terrorists like to be considered soldiers at war both because of the legitimacy they believe it brings their cause and for the status they believe it confers on them," according to Richardson.

Another goal that terrorists seek is to provoke an over-reaction, and the mother of all over-reactions has to have been the invasion of Iraq—a country that had nothing whatsoever to do with Sept. 11 attacks. Declaring war on terror may have reflected the seriousness of the Sept. 11 attacks, and of course a war puts much more power into the hands of the executive branch, the overarching goal of Vice President Dick Cheney. But in the end it was counter productive.

"We will never be able to prevent every attack," says Richardson, "but we can control our reactions to those attacks. If we keep terrorist attacks in perspective and recognize that the strongest weapons in our arsenal against terrorism are precisely the hallmarks of democracy that we value, then we can indeed contain the terrorist threat."

Telling a New Story About Terrorism

As a terrorism expert, Louise Richardson is right at home here, the site of Scotland's oldest university, which includes among its faculties the world-famous Center for the Study of Terrorism and Political Violence.

I asked Richardson if there was anything she would want to add now to her well-regarded 2006 book, "What Terrorists Want." She said that what the West needed was a "counter narrative," and that when it came to getting the message out the extremists had us "beaten hands down."

She said that it was well and good, after Sept. 11, 2001, to praise the heroic firemen and police of New York City. But if only there had been a powerful film about the Muslims who had lost their lives in the twin towers—the personal stories of Muslims who had come to America full of hope, and found it a good place to be—only to be murdered by Al Qaeda fanatics.

She said that America had a "great story to tell," but wasn't effectively telling it.

EVALUATING THE AUTHOR'S ARGUMENTS:

Greenway argues that the war on terror frames terrorists as soldiers, and this inappropriately legitimizes their cause. What do you think? Are terrorists like soldiers in a war on terror? Or are they more like criminals, as Greenway suggests? Explain your reasoning, citing evidence from the texts you have read in your answer.

Chapter 3

Can War Be Prevented?

The United Nations offers a forum for international cooperation, preventive diplomacy, arms control, human rights issues, and developmental programs aimed at preventing war.

It Is Possible to Prevent War

**Friends Committee on
National Legislation**

*"Military
force and
unilateralism
are tragically
ineffective
instruments
against the
current
threats facing
the U.S."*

In the following viewpoint the Friends Committee on National Legislation argues that the United States needs to develop a security strategy that centers around preventing, rather than starting, wars. According to the committee, at least five alternatives to war are possible: international cooperation, preventive diplomacy, arms control, human rights improvement, and sustainable development programs and practices. The committee contends that war has failed to address the threats facing the United States—it is time for the United States to switch to peaceful conflict-resolution strategies and reduce the nation's reliance on military force.

The Friends Committee on National Legislation is the lobbying arm of the Quakers. It supports arms control and disarmament and opposes the war in Iraq.

AS YOU READ, CONSIDER THE FOLLOWING QUESTIONS:
1. What does the author say are "tragically ineffective instruments" for dealing with the threats that face the United States?
2. Name at least four preventive actions former UN secretary-general Kofi Annan recommends be taken to prevent war.
3. Name three ways in which the author says improving life around the world can help nations avoid war.

If War Is Not the Answer, What Is? Peaceful Prevention of Deadly Conflict, Washington, DC: Friends Committee on National Legislation, 2005. Reproduced by permission.

I n the fall of 2002, the [George W.] Bush Administration enshrined in U.S. policy a unilateral right to take military action against "emerging threats before they are fully formed." Months later, in March 2003, against widespread global protest and without United Nations Security Council authorization, the Administration put its new policy of "preemptive" war [the Bush Doctrine] into practice by invading and occupying Iraq. The costs of the war, the path of fractured alliances left in its wake, the ongoing crisis with North Korea, and the growing realization that the war may have fueled the very threats it was intended to thwart, have demonstrated that the Bush Doctrine is far from a complete success in forging peace and security. In fact, military force and unilateralism are tragically ineffective instruments against the current threats facing the U.S. and the global community. But, if war is not the answer, then what is? . . .

Lasting Security Without War

The Bush Administration's focus on earlier response to emerging threats is an important and necessary step in U.S. policy. For too long, the world has responded too late to escalating conflicts, genocide, gross human rights abuses, failing states, the threat of terrorism, and the proliferation of weapons of mass destruction. Since the early 1990s, the international community has been facing up to and striving to overcome this "culture of reaction" by moving toward a "culture of prevention." Unfortunately, the administration's emphasis on U.S. military and economic dominance and the use of force as its main instrument of foreign policy diverges drastically from the international community's deepened understanding of how to effectively reduce conflict and prevent war.

A growing body of research is contributing to a global movement for the peaceful prevention of deadly conflict. The publishing of the report of the Carnegie Commission on Preventing Deadly Conflict in 1998, followed three years later by the release of the Secretary-General's *Report on the Prevention of Armed Conflict* and the report *Responsibility to Protect* by the International Commission on Intervention and State Sovereignty marked important steps in the world community's effort to better understand, predict, and prevent the outbreak of violent conflict.

In 2001, [UN] Secretary-General Kofi Annan called for the development of new capacities within national governments, multilateral regional organizations, civil society, and the UN to undertake genuinely preventive actions in all stages of conflict—from latent tensions to hot wars to post-conflict peacebuilding. Such actions include developing early warning systems and enhanced preventive diplomacy capacities, strengthening international law and good governance, reducing the proliferation of weapons and protecting human rights, supporting sustainable development and the fair distribution of resources, ending poverty, tackling HIV/AIDS and other public health crises, reducing ethnic tensions, building strong institutions of global civil society, and ensuring basic human security for all the world's people. . . .

Prevention, Not Preemption

The attacks of September 11, 2001 and ongoing threats of terrorism have highlighted the importance of implementing a security agenda that can better predict emerging threats, prevent their outbreak into violence, diffuse current disputes, and address the root causes of violent conflict. Rather than applying the lessons of peaceful prevention that the international community has been gathering, however, the U.S. has reverted to the outdated tools of unilateralism and overwhelming military force—instruments which promise to fuel the threats of weapons of mass destruction and terrorist attacks. Military action may stamp out some elements of a threat, but it cannot remove the roots of conflict and may instead deepen their reach.

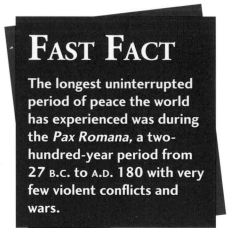

FAST FACT

The longest uninterrupted period of peace the world has experienced was during the *Pax Romana*, a two-hundred-year period from 27 B.C. to A.D. 180 with very few violent conflicts and wars.

A more effective, less costly path to national and global security is available.

Some years ago, the New York City fire department made a fundamental paradigm shift away from fire emergency response toward fire prevention. The department changed the way it approached its job and turned more energy and resources into public education, early detection systems, better building codes, and addressing some of the most persistent causes of fire. They saved lives and, over a few short years, began fighting fewer and less devastating fires. A similar shift in approach to conflict could save lives and reduce the occasion of war.

The United States Can Lead the World to Peace

The U.S. can help lead this shift. The threats of weapons of mass destruction, terrorist networks, oppressive regimes, ethnic conflict, failed states, and devastating poverty and disease can be diminished through policies and programs designed to peacefully prevent the outbreak of violence and address the root causes of conflict. As U.S. Senator Joseph Biden (DE) proposed in late July 2003, "Instead of a preemption doctrine, what we need is a prevention doctrine which diffuses problems long before they explode in our face." Such a U.S. policy framework would build on the efforts already underway within some U.S. government agencies, at the UN, among European allies, in regional organizations, and among civil society groups to develop stronger capacities for early warning, early response, and addressing root causes. It would replace the policy of "preemptive" war with one of war prevention. . . .

A New Way Forward

To effectively address current and future threats to peace and security, the U.S. needs a new security strategy for the *peaceful prevention of deadly conflict*. Such a strategy would reduce reliance on 11th hour military responses to conflict and invest in the development and early application of peaceful alternatives to war. These alternatives include:

    I.   International Cooperation and the Rule of Law
    II.   Preventive Diplomacy and Peace Operations
    III. Arms Control and Disarmament
    IV. Human Rights and Good Governance
    V.   Sustainable Development and Human Security

I. International Cooperation and the Rule of Law. Goal: Strengthen international law and multilateral cooperation to address global threats to peace and security.

- Revoke the policy of "preemptive" war;
- Support and strengthen the United Nations and other international institutions working for the peaceful prevention and settlement of conflicts;
- Work with the UN Security Council to address emerging conflicts and threats to peace and security before they reach crisis levels;
- Ratify the Rome Statute [the treaty that established the International Criminal Court] and support the International Criminal Court in bringing human rights abusers and perpetrators of crimes against humanity to justice, and
- Fulfill U.S. commitments under international treaties and work cooperatively for the strengthening of international law on arms control, human rights, the environment, and trade.

II. Preventive Diplomacy and Peace Operations. Goal: Enhance the international community's capacity to prevent the escalation of conflict, effectively respond to emerging crises, and rebuild societies shattered by war and conflict.

- Contribute annually to the UN's Trust Fund for Preventive Action;
- Invest in research and training for national, regional, and international early warning systems and early response mechanisms;
- Support the use of preventive diplomacy, including the use of mediation, arbitration, and confidence-building measures to de-escalate tensions and resolve conflicts;
- Support the creation of new international capacities for preventing and responding to conflict, including a stand-by corps of conflict resolution and prevention experts, as well as an international civilian police corps;
- Support and fund more effective civilian post-conflict reconstruction initiatives, including reconciliation and restorative justice programs.

In 2001 then–United Nations secretary-general Kofi Annan said enhancing preventive diplomacy, strengthening international law, protecting human rights, and reducing the proliferation of nuclear weapons could prevent war.

Reduce Weapons and Improve Human Rights

III. Arms Control and Disarmament. Goal: Reduce the threat of weapons of mass destruction and the escalation of conflict by enhancing international arms control and disarmament regimes.

- Renounce the first use of nuclear weapons, prohibit the development of new nuclear weapons, and stop the push for new nuclear testing in the U.S.;

- Ratify the Comprehensive Test Ban Treaty, fulfill U.S. obligations under the Non-Proliferation Treaty, and support the expansion of the Nunn-Lugar cooperative threat reduction program;
- Strengthen the Biological Weapons Convention and the Chemical Weapons Convention through enhanced monitoring and inspections;
- Work to create zones free of weapons of mass destruction in the Middle East and other regions;
- Support multilateral efforts, including the UN small arms process, to limit the spread of weapons;
- Enhance U.S. and international arms export controls, end U.S. military assistance to repressive regimes, and work internationally to end weapons flows to regions of conflict and abusive regimes.

IV. Human Rights and Good Governance. Goal: Strengthen human rights and promote good governance as foundations for stable, secure societies.

- Support active cooperation between the UN Office for the High Commissioner on Human Rights and the Security Council's Counter Terrorism Committee;
- Support the deployment of international human rights monitors in situations of conflict and emerging crises;
- Uphold U.S. commitments under international humanitarian law, including the protection of civilians in situations of conflict;
- Ratify the Convention on the Rights of the Child and work to end the use of child soldiers;
- Ratify the Convention to End Discrimination Against Women and support an increased role for women in conflict management and peacebuilding, economic life, and the political arena;
- Support programs to strengthen civil society and promote human rights awareness, democracy, transparency, accountability, and peacebuilding, particularly in pre- and post-conflict situations.

Improving Life Around the World

V. Sustainable Development and Human Security. Goal: Address the root causes of violent conflict by meeting basic human needs and promoting more equitable use of world resources.

- Increase funding for programs to integrate conflict prevention and peacebuilding within traditional development assistance;
- Increase U.S. development assistance to the world's poorest countries and work to ensure transparency and accountability in aid distribution;
- Actively work to implement the UN Millennium Development Goals, including halving global poverty by 2015, promoting environmental sustainability, and creating a global partnership for development to address issues of aid, trade, and debt;
- Provide generous and effective U.S. funding—bilaterally and through the UN—for the prevention and treatment of HIV/AIDS, malaria, and tuberculosis in Africa and other highly infected regions;
- Reduce U.S. dependence on oil by lowering consumption, developing renewable sources of energy, and promoting alternative modes of transportation;
- Work with the international community to make clean water accessible and affordable for all.

EVALUATING THE AUTHOR'S ARGUMENTS:

The Friends Committee on National Legislation offers five alternatives to war in its viewpoint. Of these alternatives, which do you believe would be the most and least effective? Rank them in order of effectiveness. Can you suggest other solutions? Try to think of at least one.

Viewpoint 2

It Is Not Always Possible to Prevent War

James V. Schall

"War is not the greatest evil, but at times the only means to prevent evil."

In the following viewpoint James V. Schall argues that sometimes war is the only valid answer to tyranny or fanaticism. He thinks that war will be necessary as long as evil, greed, and other sins exist. Furthermore, Schall argues, many of today's moral and economic problems are greater than they might have been because military force was not used when it should have been. In Schall's view, some problems can be solved only by using just, swift, warfare. He therefore concludes that the United States must always leave a military option on the table when dealing with potential threats and enemies.

Schall is a professor of government at Georgetown University.

AS YOU READ, CONSIDER THE FOLLOWING QUESTIONS:
1. What was the advice of Niccolò Machiavelli, according to Schall?
2. Why is war inevitable, according to political philosopher Herbert Deane?
3. In the author's opinion, what will be the source of the worst modern tyranny?

James V. Schall, "When War Must Be the Answer," *Policy Review*, December, 2004, pp. 59–71. Copyright © 2004 by the Board of Trustees of the Leland Stanford Junior University. Reproduced by permission.

A calm and reasonable case can and should be made for the possession and effective use of force in today's world. It is irresponsible not to plan for the necessity of force in the face of real turmoils and enemies actually present in the world. No talk of peace, justice, truth, or virtue is complete without a clear understanding that certain individuals, movements, and nations must be met with measured force, however much we might prefer to deal with them peacefully or pleasantly. Without force, many will not talk seriously at all, and some not even then. Human, moral, and economic problems are greater today for the lack of adequate military force or, more often, for the failure to use it when necessary. . . .

War Is Often the Answer

In late spring [2004], in Baltimore, I walked to the end of Chestnut Street where it meets Joppa Road. On one corner was a large official-looking residence called "Mission Helpers Center." On both sides of its entrance gate were large blue and white signs that said, "War Is Not the Answer." These placards recalled many too-simple slogans I have seen in recent years about war, often, like this one apparently, from religious sources: "War is obsolete." "War is never justified." "The answer to violence is not more violence." "War does no good." "No one wins a war." "Love, not war." "Diplomacy, not war." "Dialogue, not war." "Stop violence." "Justice, not war." "No war is legitimate." "Everyone loses in war." "War, Never Again."

When I saw the "War Is Not the Answer" sign, I said to myself, "what is the question to which war is *not* an answer?" Is there no question to which war *is* the only sensible answer? Must we be pacifists and draw no lines in the sand? Does nothing ever need defending? Can we choose not to defend what needs defending and still be honorable? If war is not the "answer," what is? How do we rid ourselves of tyrants or protect ourselves from ideologies or fanatics who attack us with their own principles and weapons, not ours?

Wars Can Be Helpful and Just

[Philosopher and politician Niccolò] Machiavelli advised that a prince should spend most of his time preparing for war. The prince was not pious except when it was useful to his staying in power. If

Fifteenth-century Italian statesman Niccolò Machiavelli believed that war is acceptable if it helps a great nation or leader obtain and maintain power.

we are this prince's neighbors, do we take no notice of his preparations? Do we give him the answer he most wants to hear from us, namely, "war is not the answer"? Those who practice this doctrine of no war make easy targets. The prince thinks war *is* an answer. It can help him in his goal of acquiring and keeping power. We may have to suffer a defeat at his hands, but we should not choose to bring one on ourselves.

Though much carnage and chaos happen in any historic war, and on every side, still we cannot conclude from this that "war is not the answer." It may not be the *only* answer. But no valid alternative to war can be a mere ungrounded velleity [inclination], a frivolous hope that nothing bad will happen no matter what we do or do not do. Any presumed alternative to war, by other supposedly more effective methods, has to stop what war seeks to prevent by its own reasoned use of measured force. The general opinion of most sensible men in most of history is that war certainly is one answer, even a reasonable answer, in the light of what would likely ensue without it. Not a few unfought wars have made things considerably worse. Not a few fought wars have made things better. The honor classically associated with war heroes is expressed in the proclamations: "Our cause is just." "Give me liberty or give me death." "Eternal vigilance is the price of liberty." "Walk softly but carry a big stick." . . .

War Can Prevent Evil

Let me cite [political philosopher] Herbert Deane's summation of Augustine's [of Hippo, also known as Saint Augustine] view of war: "Wars are inevitable as long as men and their societies are moved by avarice, greed, and lust for power, the permanent drives of sinful men. It is, therefore, self-delusion and folly to expect that a time will ever come in this world when wars will cease and 'men will beat their swords into plough-shares.'" We are asked to believe that the institutions designed to

FAST FACT

According to the *Free Republic,* as of 2009 about sixteen active wars and twelve low-level conflicts are ongoing.

replace the national state will not themselves be threats against freedom and justice. The question is whether the world and its inhabitants are better off with national states that can maintain their own judgments and forces. The answer, I believe, is that whatever the logic of the international state, its practice is too dangerous— both on the large scale and on the small.

[Political philosopher] Jean Bethke Elshtain has written, "I would argue that true international justice is defined as the equal claim of all persons, whatever their political location or condition, to having coercive force deployed in their behalf if they are victims of one or the many horrors attendant upon radical political instability." What Elshtain implies is that there is and must continue to be room for the existence and use of force that understands and works for right order. I would maintain, therefore, that much of the thinking about the obsolescence of war is itself a major contributor to war, particularly to the new kinds of war that we see in the twenty-first century. It prevents quick and effective action. Without denying that this alternative can also be abused, we can never arrive at a clear concept of the problem if the mechanisms designed to address it include it.

Justice Is Made Possible by War

Where does this leave the discussion? We are left with the need to see force and power as actual servants of justice. [Author] C.S. Lewis wrote in his essay "Why I Am Not a Pacifist:"

> It is arguable that a criminal can always be satisfactorily dealt with without the death penalty. It is certain that a whole nation cannot be prevented from taking what it wants except by war. It is almost equally certain that the absorption of certain societies by certain other societies is a great evil. The doctrine that war is always a greater evil seems to imply a materialist ethic, a belief that death and pain are the greatest evils. But I do not think they are. I think the suppression of a higher religion by a lower, of even a higher secular culture by a lower, a much greater evil . . . . The question is whether war is the greatest evil in the world, so that any state of affairs, which might result from submission, is certainly preferable. And I do not see any really cogent argument for this view.

Lewis, as usual, had it about right. War is not the greatest evil, but at times the only means to prevent evil. This is true on both a large and small scale. What we are left with is that the effective use of force is still best and most properly left in the national state. This is not the war of all against all, but the war of those who can limit terrorism and tyranny when and where it occurs. The worst modern tyranny in the

War Is Inevitable

It has been impossible to completely avoid war, as evidenced by the many violent conflicts currently underway in the world.

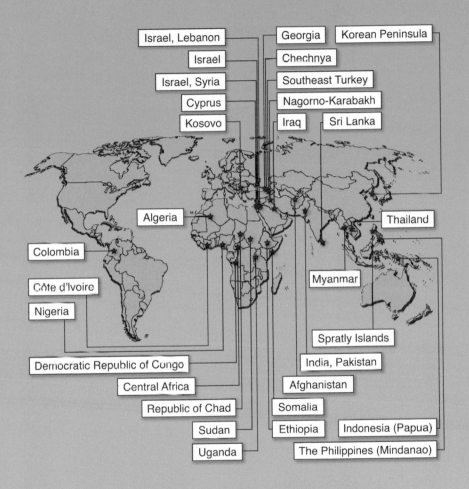

Taken from: The Military Balance, 2008.

twenty-first century will not come from armies but from their lack, from the lack of capacity and courage to use them wherever they are needed to protect justice, freedom, and truth.

The real alternative to just war cannot be viable without including the necessity and ability to deal with those who do not know or listen to reason. Law enforcement does not work unless there is a more fundamental possibility of dealing with those who are bound by no concept of legal order as we understand it. There is no alternative to just war that does not depend on and include the possibility and the exercise, when reasonable, of just war.

EVALUATING THE AUTHOR'S ARGUMENTS:

James V. Schall argues that some modern problems have worsened because military force was not used when it could have been. What problems in particular do you think Schall might be referring to, and do you agree that a military solution would be the best response?

Eliminating Nuclear Weapons Can Prevent the Threat of War

"The world can expect a nuclear or biological terror attack by 2013— unless urgent action is taken."

Dianne Feinstein

In the following viewpoint Dianne Feinstein argues that nuclear weapons are a threat to the world and must be eliminated. She explains that thousands of nuclear weapons exist all over the world, and many are not secured. She warns they could be stolen and sold to terrorists or other entities that would use them to threaten the United States and its allies. Even more dangerous are new nuclear weapons being developed by rogue nations such as Iran and North Korea. She urges the United States to lead the effort to end nuclear proliferation and guard against the threat of nuclear terrorism.

Feinstein is a Democratic senator from California.

AS YOU READ, CONSIDER THE FOLLOWING QUESTIONS:

1. According to Feinstein, which president sought the total elimination of nuclear weapons?

Dianne Feinstein, "Let's Commit to a Nuclear-Free World: Bush's Attempts to Enlarge Our Arsenal Sent Precisely the Wrong Message," *The Wall Street Journal,* January 5, 2009.

When Barack Obama becomes America's 44th president on Jan. 20 [2009], he should embrace the vision of a predecessor who declared: "We seek the total elimination one day of nuclear weapons from the face of the Earth."

That president was Ronald Reagan, and he expressed this ambitious vision in his second inaugural address on Jan. 21, 1985. It was a remarkable statement from a president who had deployed tactical nuclear missiles in Europe to counter the Soviet Union's fearsome SS-20 missile fleet.

President Reagan knew the grave threat nuclear weapons pose to humanity. He never achieved his goal, but President Obama should pick up where he left off.

Nuclear Weapons Pose a Global Threat

The Cold War is over, but there remain thousands of nuclear missiles in the world's arsenals—most maintained by the U.S. and Russia. Most are targeted at cities and are far more powerful than the bombs that destroyed Hiroshima and Nagasaki.

Today, the threat is ever more complex. As more nations pursue nuclear ambitions, the world becomes less secure, with growing odds of terrorists obtaining a nuclear weapon.

The nuclear aspirations of North Korea and Iran threaten a "cascade" of nuclear proliferation, according to a bipartisan panel led by former U.S. Defense Secretaries William J. Perry and James R. Schlesinger.

Another bipartisan panel has warned that the world can expect a nuclear or biological terror attack by 2013—unless urgent action is taken.

Nuclear weapons pose grave dangers to all nations. Seeking new weapons and maintaining massive arsenals makes no sense. It is vital that we seek a world free of nuclear weapons. The United States should lead the way, and President Obama should challenge Russian President Dmitry Medvedev to join us.

Many of the world's leading statesmen favor such an effort. They include former Soviet leader Mikhail Gorbachev, former Defense Secretary Perry, former Secretaries of State Henry Kissinger and George Shultz, and former Senate Armed Services Committee Chairman Sam Nunn.

Eight Years of Dangerous Programs

Unfortunately, for eight years the [George W.] Bush administration moved in another direction, pushing aggressive policies and new

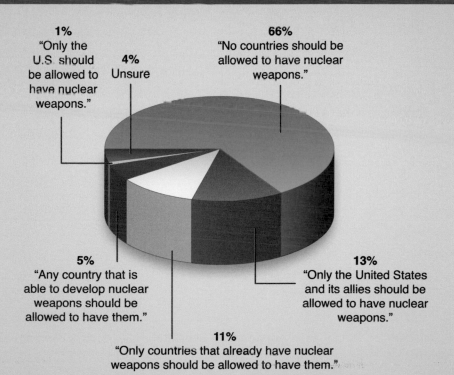

No Country Should Possess Nuclear Weapons

An Associated Press/Ipsos poll found that the majority of Americans believe that nuclear weapons are so dangerous, no country should possess them—even the United States.

"Which statement comes closest to your view?"

1%
"Only the U.S. should be allowed to have nuclear weapons."

4%
Unsure

66%
"No countries should be allowed to have nuclear weapons."

5%
"Any country that is able to develop nuclear weapons should be allowed to have them."

11%
"Only countries that already have nuclear weapons should be allowed to have them."

13%
"Only the United States and its allies should be allowed to have nuclear weapons."

Taken from: Associated Press/Ipsos poll conducted by Ipsos-Public Affairs. March 21–23, 2005.

weapons programs, threatening to reopen the nuclear door and spark the very proliferation we seek to prevent.

President Bush made it the policy of the United States to contemplate first use of nuclear weapons in response to chemical or biological attack—even against nonnuclear states.

He changed the "strategic triad"—which put nuclear weapons in a special category by themselves—by lumping them with conventional weapons in the same package of battlefield capabilities. This blurred the distinction between the two, making nuclear weapons easier to use.

And he advocated new types of weapons that could be used in a variety of circumstances against a range of targets, advancing the notion that nuclear weapons have utility beyond deterrence.

FAST FACT

About twenty-seven thousand nuclear weapons exist worldwide, but just fifty of these, according to the *New Internationalist*, would be enough to kill 200 million people.

Dangerous Developments

Mr. Bush then sought funding for new weapons programs, including:

- A 100-kiloton "bunker buster" that scientists say would not destroy enemy bunkers as advertised, but would have spewed enough radiation to kill one million people.
- The Advanced Concepts Initiative, including developing a low-yield nuclear weapon for tactical battlefield use.
- The Modern Pit Facility, a factory that could produce up to 450 plutonium triggers a year—even though scientists say America's nuclear triggers will be good for years.
- Pushing to reduce time-to-test readiness at the Nevada Test Site in half—to 18 months—signaling intent to resume testing, which would have broken a test moratorium in place since 1992.
- A new nuclear warhead, called the Reliable Replacement Warhead, which could spark a new global arms race.

I opposed these programs, and Congress slashed or eliminated funding for them.

But President Bush had sent dangerous signals world-wide. Allies could conclude if the United States sought new nuclear weapons, they should too. Adversaries could conclude acquiring nuclear weapons would be insurance against preemptive U.S. attack.

We Must Eliminate Nuclear Weapons

Here's how President-elect Obama can change course. By law he must set forth his views on nuclear weapons in U.S. national security strategy, in his Nuclear Posture Review, by 2010. In it, he should commit the U.S. to working with Russia to lower each nation's arsenal of deployed nuclear warheads below the 1,700–2,200 the Moscow Treaty already calls for by 2013.

It would be a strong step toward reducing our bloated arsenals, and signal the world that we have changed course.

I was 12 when atomic bombs flattened Hiroshima and Nagasaki, killing more than 200,000 people. The horrific images that went around the world have stayed with me all my life.

During his second inaugural address on January 21, 1985, President Ronald Reagan became the first American president to call for total elimination of nuclear weapons.

Today, there are enough nuclear weapons to destroy the world hundreds of times. And we now face the chilling prospect of nuclear terrorism.

The bottom line: We must recognize nuclear weapons for what they are—not a deterrent, but a grave and gathering threat to humanity. As president, Barack Obama should dedicate himself to their world-wide elimination.

EVALUATING THE AUTHOR'S ARGUMENTS:

Dianne Feinstein chairs the Senate Committee on Intelligence, which oversees civilian and military agencies. Do you think this background increases the credibility of her argument? Explain why or why not.

Viewpoint 4

Unilateral Nuclear Disarmament Will Destabilize Regions

Barry M. Blechman

"Significant unilateral reduction would be a terrible mistake. The cuts . . . would create new problems that could, ironically, increase the risk of proliferation."

In the following viewpoint Barry M. Blechman argues that it would be unwise for the United States to unilaterally reduce its arsenal of nuclear weapons. He warns that doing so would make America and its allies more vulnerable to potential enemies and would do nothing to contain proliferation. America's vast nuclear arsenal discourages other countries from attacking it, he explains. If the United States did not have such weapons, it would be more vulnerable to attack and less able to make other countries do what it wants. Blechman also says that nuclear weapons cuts would weaken the United States' ability to negotiate weapons treaties with other nations. He concludes that if the United States wants to reduce the number of nuclear weapons worldwide while keeping itself and its allies safe, it should do so slowly and only if other nations are getting rid of their weapons, too.

Barry M. Blechman, "Don't Reduce the U.S. Nuclear Arsenal Unilaterally: We Need Levers to Move the World Toward Disarmament," Henry L. Stimson Center, www.stimson.org, January 21, 2008. Copyright © 2007–2009 The Henry L. Stimson Center. Reproduced by permission.

Blechman is the cofounder of the Henry L. Stimson Center, a public policy institute that aims to improve international peace and security.

AS YOU READ, CONSIDER THE FOLLOWING QUESTIONS:
1. What nations does Blechman say have not developed nuclear weapons because the United States has promised to protect them with American ones?
2. What does the term "nuclear umbrella" mean in the context of the viewpoint?
3. U.S. and Russian arsenals constitute what amount of the world's nuclear weapons, as stated by the author?

President [Barack] Obama does not lack advice on the nuclear policies he should pursue. Six projects, at least, are providing such recommendations. Prominent among them are suggestions that the US should reduce its nuclear arsenal unilaterally, eliminating weapons that most observers agree are no longer needed for military purposes. Unilateral cuts, it is argued, would set a good example for other countries and would strengthen US non-proliferation credentials, making it easier to persuade Iran and North Korea to give up their aspirations for nuclear weapons and permitting the US to enter the 2010 Non-proliferation Treaty (NPT) Review Conference from a position of strength. Recommendations differ on the size of the cut, but most believe that around 1,000 weapons would provide all the nuclear deterrence the US needs—and then some.

America's Nukes Keep the Peace

Such a significant unilateral reduction would be a terrible mistake. The cuts would not accomplish the goals claimed for them and would create new problems that could, ironically, increase the risk of proliferation. Most importantly, they would diminish opportunities to negotiate mutual reductions in US and Russian arsenals that could eventually lead to a nuclear-free world.

The US has long sought to prevent its allies from acquiring nuclear weapons by committing itself to their security, including an assurance to counter any nuclear threat against them. Many NATO [North Atlantic Treaty Organization] members, Japan, South Korea, and Taiwan, have relinquished nuclear weapon programs in exchange for these security guarantees. In the 1990s, Belarus, Kazakhstan, and Ukraine were also persuaded to give up the nuclear arms they had inherited from the Soviet Union, in part by implied nuclear guarantees.

A staff member of the Comprehensive Test Ban Treaty Organization works at the operations desk at its headquarters in Vienna. The organization has built an international monitoring system to detect secret nuclear tests, and the author of this viewpoint urges President Barack Obama to utilize the system to prevent nuclear proliferation and promote unilateral disarmament.

The State of Nuclear Weapons Today

Because they feel they need them to enhance their security, many countries keep and pursue nuclear weapons programs.

Nuclear Powers

Country	Year Acquired	Estimated Number of Nuclear Warheads
United States	1945	4,075–5,535
Russia	1949	5,200–8,800
United Kingdom	1952	160
France	1960	350
China	1964	160–400
India	1974	100–200
Israel*	1979	100–140
Pakistan	1998	60
North Korea	2006	0–10

*Israel has never admitted to possessing nuclear weapons, so its stockpile and date acquired are speculative.

Countries Believed to Be Pursuing Nuclear Weapons

Country	State of Program
Iran	The International Atomic Energy (IAEA) and the United States have accused Iran of undertaking secret nuclear activities to produce fissile material for bombs. Iran claims its nuclear endeavors are for peaceful energy purposes.
Syria	Syria has signed the Nuclear Proliferation Treaty, which prohibits it from developing nuclear weapons. However, in September 2007, Israel conducted an airstrike on what some experts say may have been the construction site of a nuclear research reactor.

Taken from: Compiled by the editor from several sources.

For such guarantees to be credible the US must at least maintain numerical parity [equivalence] with the nuclear forces of potential enemies. Significant unilateral reductions by the US would greatly worry states concerned about Russian nuclear forces; these include newer Eastern European NATO members, Ukraine, and even older NATO members if the cuts were large enough. Key Asian states are concerned about China's growing nuclear capabilities and North Korea's fledgling nuclear arsenal. While even reduced US nuclear forces would still greatly exceed China's and North Korea's, allied countries would wonder if they could depend on the US "nuclear umbrella" indefinitely. At a minimum, these concerns could cause grave alliance difficulties; conceivably, they could lead some to pursue their own nuclear capabilities. Another regional effect of a sufficiently deep cut might be China's con-clusion that it could easily match US nuclear capabilities. Such a development could lead to sig-nificant problems in the event of a Taiwan or Korean crisis.

Nuclear Weapons Keep Other Countries in Check

Unilateral reductions of the mag-nitude being discussed also would reduce President Obama's lever-age with Russia when negotiating potential mutual restraints on arsenals. Russian and US arsenals comprise roughly 95 percent of the world's nuclear weapons. It is evident that deeper reductions on their part are an essential next step on the road to eliminating nuclear weapons world-wide. But why should Moscow agree to limits on its own forces when the US is already stripping its arsenal unilaterally? Russian military doctrine values short-range, or "tactical" nuclear weapons to offset Western conventional superiority. Persuading Russia to include these shorter range weapons in future agreements will be difficult without having anything significant to trade.

> # FAST FACT
>
> Since the advent of nuclear weapons, military strategy has featured a concept called "mutual assured destruction," in which it is believed war can be averted if both parties have nuclear weapons—the threat of their own destruction if they attack is believed to be enough to prevent them from using their weapons.

Nor would a unilateral reduction help the US contain proliferation. Iran and North Korea will pursue their weapon programs depending on broad strategic, economic, and political considerations, whether the US has 1,000 or 5,000 weapons. In either case, they would be helplessly outnumbered and would depend on a US unwillingness to sustain even a single nuclear blast on its territory to deter American involvement in a regional crisis.

The United States Should Work with Other Nations to Reduce Nuclear Weapons

There would be no gain at the NPT Review Conference either. The US nuclear stockpile has been reduced by three-fourths since 1989, but there is nary a mention of that in the records of the NPT proceedings—other than those inserted by US representatives. Instead, the nations dissatisfied with the treaty focus solely on the Bush Administration's attempts to develop two new warheads, which have been denied repeatedly by the Congress.

President Obama also should be aware of the political implications. The announcement by a new president that he is making significant unilateral reductions in US nuclear forces, in the hope the Russians will follow suit, would play into the hands of those seeking to tar him and his party as "weak on defense."

President Obama has embraced the vision of a world free of nuclear weapons. There are no shortcuts. The US can strengthen its position in the NPT Review Conference by ratifying the Comprehensive Test Ban Treaty and persuading China, India and other nations to follow suit. The Obama Administration can regain the high ground in talks with Iran and North Korea by dropping the distinction between "good" and "bad" nuclear caretakers and pursuing the elimination of nuclear weapons by all nations. And it needs to restart the dialogue with Russia, seeking common ground on missile defenses, a quick extension of the START [Strategic Arms Reduction Treaty] and Moscow Agreement, and the beginning of doubtlessly difficult negotiations for a comprehensive agreement to significantly reduce both sides' total stock of nuclear warheads. At that point, the United States and Russia could turn to the rest of the world and say, with a straight face and clear eye, "Comrades, now let us discuss a treaty to rid the world of all nuclear weapons, weapons which serve no purpose but which threaten all civilized life."

EVALUATING THE AUTHORS' ARGUMENTS:

Barry M. Blechman argues that reducing America's supply of nuclear weapons weakens it. How do you think Dianne Feinstein, author of the previous viewpoint, would respond to this argument? Write two or three sentences summarizing her potential response.

Facts About War

Editor's note: These facts can be used in reports or papers to reinforce or add credibility when making important points or claims.

The War on Terrorism

A 2009 NBC News/*Wall Street Journal* poll asked Americans whether they believed that as a country, America was more safe, as safe, or less safe than before the war on terror was begun. Americans said:

- 29 percent felt more safe
- 40 percent felt about as safe
- 28 percent felt less safe
- 3 percent were unsure

According to the U.S. State Department, in 2008 there were:

- 44 active terrorist groups

- 11,770 attacks worldwide
- 8,438 attacks resulting in death, injury, or kidnapping of at least one person
- 5,067 attacks resulting in the death of at least one individual
- 6,703 attacks resulting in the death of zero individuals
- 2,889 attacks resulting in the death of only one individual
- 235 attacks resulting in the death of at least 10 individuals
- 4,888 attacks resulting in the injury of at least one individual
- 1,125 attacks resulting in the kidnapping of at least one individual

- 54,747 people killed, injured, or kidnapped as a result of terrorism
- 15,765 people worldwide killed as a result of terrorism
- 34,124 people worldwide injured as a result of terrorism
- 4,858 people worldwide kidnapped as a result of terrorism

- Compared to 2007, the number of terrorist attacks decreased by 18 percent in 2008. However, deaths due to terrorism increased by 30 percent in 2008.

- The most attacks occurred in the Near East.
- The Near East and South Asia had the greater number of fatalities from terrorism—75 percent of the 235 high-casualty attacks (those that killed 10 or more people) in 2008 occurred there.

- The Taliban, more than any other group, claimed credit for the largest number of attacks and the highest fatality totals.

- Well over 50 percent of the 2008 terrorist victims were Muslims, and most were victims of attacks in Iraq, Pakistan, and Afghanistan.

According to a 2008 *Foreign Policy* poll of more than 100 policy experts:
- 70 percent say the U.S. is losing the war on terror
- 12 percent say the U.S. is winning the war on terror
- 9 percent are unsure

Religion and Warfare
According to the *New Internationalist:*
- Religion played a significant role in the following major wars (listed in the order of how religious they were):
    - Arab Conquests 632–732
    - The Crusades 1097–1291
    - al Qaeda terror war 1992–
    - Reformation wars 1562–1598
    - U.S. and allied invasion of Iraq 2003–
    - Afghanistan's anti-Soviet war 1979–1989
    - Thirty Years' War 1618–1648
    - Moghul Conquest of India 1503–1529
    - Spanish Conquests in North and South America 1492–1541
    - American Revolution 1775–1783
    - Sudan Civil War 1983–
    - American Indian wars 1860–1890
    - European colonial wars, Africa, Asia, Pacific 1870–1945
    - Spanish Civil War 1936–1939
    - Arab-Israeli wars 1947–1982
    - U.S.-Soviet Cold War 1948–1991

- Fall of Constantinople 1453
- Seven Years' War 1756–1763
- Second World War 1939–1945
- Northern Ireland 1968–1998
- Iran-Iraq War 1980–1988
- Bosnia 1994–1995
- Chechen wars 1994 and 1999
- U.S. and Allied invasion of Afghanistan 2001–
- Many smaller scale conflicts, such as Hindu-Muslim clashes in India (claiming some 2,000 lives in 2002) and Christian-Muslim clashes in Indonesia and in Nigeria.

- Christian states have killed more Jews and Muslims than Muslim states have killed Christians or Jews.
- In the past thousand years more devastating wars among Christian states fighting each other have occurred than between Christian and Muslim states.
- Two atheistic states—Josef Stalin's Russia and Mao Zedong's China—have perpetrated more mass murder than any state dominated by a religious faith. Stalinism cost the Soviet Union between 9 and 60 million lives; Maoism cost China between 30 and 40 million.
- In killing six million Jews in the Holocaust, Nazi leader Adolf Hitler was responsible for the single most devastating genocide in history of a group identified by their religion and race.

According to the British Broadcasting Service, religion has been the basis for many peaceful social justice movements and organizations, including:
- the antislavery movement
- the black civil rights movement
- antiapartheid movement in South Africa
- Mahatma Gandhi's nonviolent campaign in India, which drew in part on Hinduism
- the Islamic practice of *zakat* (or alms tax) whereby 2.5% of income is donated for those in need
- humanitarian agencies and charities of various denominations
- some religions—such as Buddhism, Jainism and Quakerism—that have nonviolence as a central tenet

Climate Change and War

According to the Intergovernmental Panel on Climate Change (IPCC):

- During the twentieth century the global average surface temperature increased by about 0.6°C.
- Global sea levels increased about 15 to 20 centimeters.
- The average global temperature will rise another 1.1° to 5.4°C (2.0° to 9.8 °F) by 2100.
- The Earth's climate will change faster in the one hundred years between 2000 and 2100 than in the last ten thousand years.
- A hundred million people live within 3 feet (1m) of sea level. Most of the global population lives in coastal areas that could flood should sea levels rise dramatically.

According to a 2008 Harris poll:

- Forty percent of Americans think that global warming could threaten national security if it continues unchecked.

Nuclear Weapons and War

Nine nations possess nuclear weapons:

- the United States (since 1945)
- Russia (1949)
- the United Kingdom (1952)
- France (1960)
- China (1964)
- India (1974)
- Pakistan (1998)
- North Korea (2006)
- Israel (though it has never admitted possessing them, Israel is believed to have developed nuclear weapons in 1979)

About forty nations are suspected to have enough nuclear materials to either build bombs or to start nuclear weapons programs.

Ninety-five percent of the more than twenty-seven thousand existing nuclear weapons belong to either the United States or Russia.

According to a 2008 *Foreign Policy* poll of more than one hundred policy experts:

- 28 percent believe Iran is likely to transfer nuclear weapons materials to terrorists.
- 69 percent believe Pakistan is likely to transfer nuclear weapons materials to terrorists.

A 2005 Associated Press/Ipsos poll found that Americans hold the following opinions on nuclear weapons:

- 66 percent said no countries should be allowed to have nuclear weapons,
- 13 percent said only the United States and its allies should be allowed to have nuclear weapons;
- 11 percent said only countries that already have nuclear weapons should be allowed to have them;
- 5 percent said any country that is able to develop nuclear weapons should be allowed to have them;
- 1 percent said only the United States should have nuclear weapons;
- 4 percent were unsure.

Organizations to Contact

The editors have compiled the following list of organizations concerned with the issues debated in this book. The descriptions are derived from materials provided by the organizations. All have publications or information available for interested readers. The list was compiled on the date of publication of the present volume; the information provided here may change. Be aware that many organizations take several weeks or longer to respond to queries, so allow as much time as possible.

Carnegie Endowment for International Peace (CEIP)
1779 Massachusetts Ave. NW
Washington, DC 20036
(202) 483-7600
fax: (202) 483-1840
e-mail: info@ccip.org
Web site: www.ceip.org

This private, nonprofit organization is dedicated to advancing cooperation between nations and promoting active international engagement by the United States. It publishes the quarterly journal *Foreign Policy*, a magazine of international politics and economics that is published in several languages and reaches readers in more than 120 countries.

Cato Institute
1000 Massachusetts Ave. NW
Washington, DC 20001-5403
(202) 842-0200
fax: (202) 842-3490
Web site: www.cato.org

CATO is a libertarian public policy research foundation dedicated to peace and limited government intervention in foreign affairs. It publishes numerous reports and periodicals, including *Policy Analysis* and

Cato Policy Review, both of which discuss U.S. policy in regional conflicts. Its Web site offers a searchable database of institute articles, news, and commentary.

Center for Defense Information (CDI)
1779 Massachusetts Ave. NW, Ste. 615
Washington, DC 20036
(202) 332-0600
fax: (202) 462-4559
e-mail: cdi@igc.apc.org
Web site: www.cdi.org

CDI was founded by retired senior military officers to serve as an independent monitor of the military. It focuses on all matters relating to U.S. military, foreign policy, spending, and weapons. To encourage the intellectual freedom of its staff, the center does not hold organizational positions on public policy issues. It publishes the weekly journal *Defense Monitor.*

Center for Security Policy
1920 L St. NW, Ste. 210
Washington, DC 20036
(202) 835-9077
fax: (202) 835-9066
email: info@centerforsecuritypolicy.org
Web site: www.centerforsecuritypolicy.org

The Center for Security Policy is a nonprofit, nonpartisan organization committed to the philosophy of promoting international peace through American strength. It accomplishes this goal by stimulating and informing national and international policy debates, in particular, those involving regional, defense, economic, financial, and technology developments that bear upon the security of the United States. Its Web site features a wealth of papers related to military and defense matters.

Center for Strategic and International Studies (CSIS)
1800 K St. NW
Washington, DC 20006
(202) 887-0200

fax: (202) 775-3199

Web site: www.csis.org

CSIS is a public policy research institution that specializes in the areas of U.S. domestic and foreign policy, national security, and economic policy. The center analyzes world crisis situations and recommends U.S. military and defense policies. Its Web site has a searchable database of news, articles, testimony, and reports.

Coalition for the International Criminal Court (CICC)

c/o WFM, 777 UN Plaza

New York, NY 10017

(212) 687-2176

fax: (212) 599-1332

e-mail: cicc@iccnow.org

Web site: www.iccnow.org

CICC is a network of over two thousand nongovernmental organizations that advocate for a fair, effective, and independent International Criminal Court (ICC). CICC publishes the semiannual *ICC Monitor*, recent issues of which are available on its Web site. The CICC Web site also publishes fact sheets and statements in support of the ICC.

Council on Foreign Relations

58 E. 68th St.

New York, NY 10021

(212) 434-9400

fax: (212) 434-9800

Web site: www.cfr.org

This organization specializes in foreign affairs and studies the international aspects of American political and economic policies and problems. Its journal *Foreign Affairs*, published five times a year, includes analyses of current conflicts around the world. Its Web site publishes editorials, interviews, and articles.

Crimes of War Project

1205 Lamont St. NW

Washington, DC 20010

(202) 494-3834

fax: (202) 387-6858

e-mail: office@crimesofwar.org
Web site: www.crimesofwar.org

A collaboration of journalists, lawyers, and scholars dedicated to raising public awareness of the laws of war. The project publishes *Crimes of War* magazine, recent issues of which are available on its Web site, as are essays and reports.

Global Exchange
2017 Mission, #303
San Francisco, CA 94110
(415) 255-7296
fax: (415) 255-7498
e-mail: info@globalexchange.org
Web site: www.globalexchange.org

This human rights organization exposes economic and political injustice around the world. It supports education, activism, and a noninterventionist U.S. foreign policy.

Heritage Foundation
214 Massachusetts Ave. NE
Washington, DC 20002-4999
(202) 546-4400
fax: (202) 546-8328
e-mail: pubs@heritage.org
Web site: www.heritage.org

The Heritage Foundation advocates limited government and the free-market system. The foundation publishes the quarterly *Policy Review* as well as monographs, books, and papers supporting U.S. noninterventionism. Its Web site contains news and commentary and searchable databases.

Hoover Institution on War, Revolution and Peace
Stanford University
Stanford, CA 94305-6010
(650) 723-1754
fax: (650) 723-1687
e-mail: horaney@hoover.stanford.edu
Web site: www.hoover.stanford.edu

This public policy research center is devoted to studying politics, economics, and international affairs. It publishes books on a wide range of national and international policy issues that may be purchased through the Hoover Press or read online.

Human Rights Watch
350 Fifth Ave., 34th Floor
New York, NY 10118-3299
(212) 290-4700
fax: (212) 736-1300
e-mail: hrwnyc@hrw.org
Web site: www.hrw.org

Founded in 1978, this nongovernmental organization conducts systematic investigations of human rights abuses in countries around the world. It publishes many books and reports on specific countries and issues as well as annual reports, recent selections of which are available on its Web site.

International Committee of the Red Cross
Washington Delegation
2100 Pennsylvania Ave. NW, Ste. 5454
Washington, DC 20038
(202) 293-9430
Web site: www.icrc.org

The ICRC works to protect the lives and dignity of victims of war and internal violence. It directs and coordinates international relief activities and promotes humanitarian law and principles. Its Web site includes the text of the Geneva Conventions, subsequent protocols, and articles and reports on recent issues related to its mission.

Nuclear Age Peace Foundation
1187 Coast Village Rd. Ste. 1, PMB 121
Santa Barbara, CA 93108-2794
(805) 965-3443
fax: (805) 568-0466
Web site: www.wagingpeace.org

Founded in 1982, the Nuclear Age Peace Foundation, a nonprofit, nonpartisan international education and advocacy organization, initiates and supports worldwide efforts to abolish nuclear weapons, to strengthen international law and institutions, to use technology responsibly and sustainably, and to empower youth to create a more peaceful world.

RAND Corporation (RAND)
1700 Main St.
Santa Monica, CA 90407-2138
(310) 393-0411
fax: (310) 451-6960
Web site: www.rand.org

RAND is a nonprofit institution that attempts to improve public policy through research and analysis. It was created at the urging of its original sponsor, the U.S. Air Force (then the Army Air Forces), and from its inception has focused on the nation's most pressing policy problems.

Resource Center for Nonviolence
515 Broadway
Santa Cruz, CA 95060
(831) 423-1626
fax: (831) 423-8716
e-mail: information@rcnv.org
Web site: www.rcnv.org

The Resource Center for Nonviolence was founded in 1976 and promotes nonviolence as a force for personal and social change. The center provides speakers, workshops, leadership development, and nonviolence training programs. Its Web site publishes editorials, essays, news articles, and reports.

United for Peace and Justice (UFPJ)
PO Box 607 Times Square Station
New York, NY 10108
(212) 868-5545
Web site: www.unitedforpeace.org

UFPJ opposes preemptive wars of aggression and rejects any drive to expand U.S. control over other nations and strip Americans of rights at home under the cover of fighting terrorism and spreading democracy. It rejects the use of war and racism to concentrate power in the hands of the few. The UFPJ Web site publishes recent antiwar events, news articles, and essays.

For Further Reading

Books

Allawi, Ali A. *The Occupation of Iraq: Winning the War, Losing the Peace.* New Haven, CT: Yale University Press, 2008. A former senior minister in the Iraqi government provides an insider's account of the nascent Iraqi government following the American invasion.

Aslan, Reza. *How to Win a Cosmic War: God, Globalization, and the End of the War on Terror.* New York: Random House, 2009. A leading American analyst explores how war has plagued every religious tradition and nation.

Bergman, Ronen. *The Secret War with Iran: The 30-Year Clandestine Struggle Against the World's Most Dangerous Terrorist Power.* New York: Free Press, 2008. Makes the case that Iran is the biggest threat to U.S. security.

Campbell, Kurt M. *Climatic Cataclysm: The Foreign Policy and National Security Implications of Climate Change.* Washington, DC: Brookings Institution, 2008. Creates three scenarios about the way the peoples of the world may come to live as the result of climate change at various levels of severity.

Engel, Richard. *War Journal: My Five Years in Iraq.* New York: Simon & Schuster, 2008. NBC News's Middle East bureau chief offers an unvarnished and emotional account of five years in Iraq.

Mamdani, Mahmood. *Saviors and Survivors: Darfur, Politics, and the War on Terror.* New York: Pantheon, 2009. Looks at the crisis in Darfur within the context of the history of Sudan and examines the world's response to that crisis.

Nasr, Vali. *The Shia Revival: How Conflicts with Islam Will Shape the Future.* New York: W.W. Norton and Company, 2006. Argues that the Shia peoples in the Shia Crescent (an area that includes Iran) are gaining strength since the fall of Saddam Hussein.

Norman, James R. *The Oil Card: Global Economic Warfare in the 21st Century.* Waterville, OR: TrineDay, 2008. Discusses how oil pricing and availability have a long history of being employed as economic weapons by the United States.

Pearce, Fred. *When the Rivers Run Dry: Water—the Defining Crisis of the Twenty-first Century*. Boston: Beacon, 2007. Argues that a worldwide water shortage is the most fearful looming environmental crisis that will force countries to go to war.

Ricks, Thomas E. *Fiasco: The American Military Adventure in Iraq, 2003 to 2005*. New York: Penguin, 2007. A history of the war in Iraq by a Pentagon correspondent for the *Washington Post*.

Rutledge, Ian. *Addicted to Oil: America's Relentless Drive for Energy Security*. New York: I.B. Tauris, 2006. Provides a sweeping account of the forces, policies, and personalities that drive America's unending pursuit of foreign petroleum.

Scheuer, Michael. *Imperial Hubris: Why the West Is Losing the War on Terror*. Dulles, VA: Potomac, 2007. A critique of the war on terror.

Singer, P.W. *Wired for War: The Robotics Revolution and Conflict in the 21st Century*. New York: Penguin, 2009. Suggests that robotics promises to be the most comprehensive instrument of change in war since the introduction of gunpowder.

Zubrin, Robert. *Energy Victory: Winning the War on Terror by Breaking Free of Oil*. Amherst, NY: Prometheus, 2007. Argues for a biofuel-based approach to the problem of oil use in the world.

Periodicals

Austin, Greg, Todd Kranock, and Thom Oommen, *God and War: An Audit & an Exploration*," British Broadcasting Company, 2004. http://news.bbc.co.uk/2/shared/spl/hi/world/04/war_audit_pdf/pdf/war_audit.pdf.

Bell, Daniel M., Jr. "Can a War Against Terror Be Just? Or, What Is War Good For?" *Cross Currents*, Spring 2006. www.crosscurrents.org/Bellspring2006.pdf.

Benderman, Monica. "How to Stop a War," CommonDreams.org, February 11, 2006. www.commondreams.org/views06/0211-27.htm.

Brietbart, Peter. "Sometimes War Is a Necessary Evil—but Let's Hope Obama Will Find Alternatives," *Badger* (United Kingdom), November 10, 2008. www.thebadgeronline.co.uk/comment/

sometimes-war-is-a-necessary-evil-but-lets-hope-obama-will-find-alternatives.

Carafano, James Jay, and Mackenzie Eaglen, "Four Percent for Freedom: Maintaining Robust National Security Spending," Heritage Foundation, Executive Memorandum No. 1023, April 10, 2007. www.heritage.org/Research/NationalSecurity/em1023.cfm.

Clark, Wesley. "Averting the Next Gulf War: The Troop 'Surge' in Iraq Is Also a Signal to Iran—but Stopping Tehran's Nukes for Good Will Require a Different Kind of Leverage," *Washington Monthly*, April 2007.

Department of Energy and Department of Defense, "National Security and Nuclear Weapons in the 21st Century," September 2008. www.defenselink.mil/news/nuclearweaponspolicy.pdf.

Douthat, Ross. "Just War and Modern Warfare," *Atlantic*, January 5, 2009. http://rossdouthat.theatlantic.com/archives/2009/01/just_war_and_modern_warfare.php.

Economist, "Streams of Blood, or Streams of Peace; Rivers and Conflict," May 3, 2008.

Guitta, Olivier. "Use of the Energy Weapon to Avert War," *Middle East Times*, July 14, 2008. www.metimes.com/International/2008/07/14/use_of_the_energy_weapon_to_avert_war/3764.

Higgs, Robert. "The Trillion-Dollar Defense Budget Is Already Here," Independent Institute, March 15, 2007. www.independent.org/newsroom/article.asp?id=1941.

Loy, David R. "The New Holy War Between Good and Evil," *Tikkun*, November/December 2007.

Mueller, John. "Is There Still a Terrorist Threat? The Myth of the Omnipresent Enemy," *Foreign Affairs*, September/October 2006. www.foreignaffairs.org/20060901facomment85501-p0/john-mueller/is-there-still-a-terrorist-threat-the-myth-of-the-omnipresent-enemy.html.

Omestad, Thomas. "Nuclear Weapons for All? The Risks of a New Scramble for the Bomb," *U.S. News & World Report*, January 15, 2009.

Perkovich, George. "Abolishing Nuclear Weapons: Why the United States Should Lead," Carnegie Endowment for International Peace, October 2008. www.carnegieendowment.org/files/abolishing_nuclear_weapons.pdf.

Robbins, Carla Anne. "Thinking the Unthinkable: A World Without Nuclear Weapons," *New York Times*, June 30, 2008. www.nytimes.com/2008/06/30/opinion/30mon4.html.

Schmitt, Gary J., and Reuel Marc Gerecht, "How the West Can Avert War with Iran," American Enterprise Institute, February 14, 2007. www.aei.org/publications/pubID.25623,filter.all/pub_detail.asp.

Shultz, George, Henry Kissinger, Sam Nunn, and William J. Perry, "Toward a Nuclear-Free World," *Wall Street Journal*, January 15, 2008. http://online.wsj.com/article/SB120036422673589947.html?mod=opinion_main_commentaries.

von Mises, Ludwig. "Economic Causes of War," Ludwig von Mises Institute, May 14, 2008. http://mises.org/story/2949.

Web Sites

American Red Cross (www.redcross.org). A nonprofit organization that brings medical and other relief supplies to war zones and other disaster areas.

The Anti-War Commitee (AWC) (www.antiwarcommittee.org). Organizes protests, educational events, and other related activities to oppose war.

Children of War (http://thechildrenofwar.org/web1). An organization dedicated to educating and training children whose lives have been affected by the war in Afghanistan.

GoArmy.com (www.goarmy.com). The recruiting site for the U.S. Army. Contains stories of real soldiers who have fought in combat and offers information for anyone considering enlisting in the U.S. military.

Iraq Veterans Against the War (http://ivaw.org). A Web site founded by veterans of the Iraq War. The site aims to give a voice to active-duty service people and veterans who are against the war but are under various pressures to remain silent.

Stop the War Machine (www.stopthewarmachine.org). This Web site works to educate the American people about the reality of

President Dwight Eisenhower's warning about a global empire based on war. Contains articles and links to promote peace and democracy.

U.S. Department of Defense (www.defenselink.mil). The Department of Defense provides the military forces needed to deter war and to protect the security of the United States. The DoD's Web site contains recent speeches, news alerts, and press releases on defense-related matters.

U.S. Department of Veterans Affairs (www.va.gov). Contains information, articles, and press releases regarding veterans' issues of all wars fought by the United States.

U.S. Veterans.com (www.usveterans.com). A privately run Web site where veterans from all wars can locate each other. Contains links to popular films and books related to the military.

Index

Picture Credits

Thaier Al-Sudani/Reuters/Landov, 33
AP Images, 10, 14, 28, 65, 80, 85, 101, 111, 125, 129
Jon Arnold Images Ltd./Alamy, 40
Shen Hong/Xinhua/Landov, 105
Hossein Fatemi/UPI/Landov, 19
Imagno/Hulton Archive/Getty Images, 51, 116
Stan Meagher/Hulton Archive/Getty Images, 55
Popperfoto/Getty Images, 74
Goran Tomasevic/Reuters/Landov, 62
Jay Westcott/*Bloomberg News*/Landov, 97
Steve Zmina, 13, 21, 27, 35, 42, 56–57, 75, 79, 87, 92, 119, 123, 130